Real Da Vinci code. Occu...

By Dick Shegalov

Foreword

The task that the author of this book took upon himself is so monumental that if the author himself was in the shoes of the reader of this book 15 years ago, he would not have believed that such things are possible in the modern world. It's hard to believe that in the XXI century magic formulas, alchemical symbols and numerology, everything that seemed to have sunk into oblivion several hundred years ago are still used, and now that they seemed to be limited only to a narrow circle of esoteric amateurs who could in no way influence the political course of governments or have impact on the media space. In order to show that this is not the case at all, I must abundantly supply this book with illustrations and stacks of films, so as not to plunge even a favorably inclined reader into an endless search for confirmation of the compiled information. I will do it for you myself, as I understand perfectly that any person could not see all the feature films, remember all the scenes from there, and, also remember the dates of births and the names of all the actors. It would be like trying to read a book in a foreign language with a dictionary. The author realizes that, all of the following may seem so improbable and accidental to the reader that any of my statements, at least at the initial stage, will require the most ponderous evidence and clear illustrations from my part. I would not like to appear as an average "conspiracy theorist" who builds far-reaching conclusions based on false, absolutely unverified or unverifiable information. I am not going to do such conclusions until I have absolutely indisputable proofs, and not vague references to "an anonymous source in the White House" or "Hollywood insider." I will not refer to any closed sources, for I myself have never had any access to them. I will present you with a simple and reliable method of digital information analysis, which is based on my own knowledge of the history of religions, occultism and religious symbolism, a method that any of the readers can apply at home and double-check any of my statements. In other words, I take on the role of the real Professor Langdon from the novels of Dan Brown, but with one huge difference. I do not set out to write an entertaining but factually inaccurate fiction book. I hope that in the future, the reader, armed with my method, will go much further than me and will solve for himself other tasks that for the time being I myself have not been able to.

Chapter I Power and Occultism

Since time immemorial, people in power have sought the help of otherworldly forces. This happened, both within the framework of official religious beliefs of those times, and far beyond. The Russian Tsars and American Presidents were no exception. For example, Tsar Ivan IV the Terrible kept with him as a doctor the Westphalian Eloisius Bomelius. The Pskov chronicles reasonably called Bomelius "wise magician". He prepared for the king poisons, from which the victims "died at the appointed time." Tsar Ivan trusted so much his doctor and adviser that he even discussed with him the plan of marriage to Elizabeth of England. It is known that Aloisius Bomelius was also an astrologer. People often could watch him on the bell tower of the Kremlin Church of St. John Climacus, where he surveyed the location of the heavenly bodies, terrifying with his sight the common people.

Despite many denunciations of him, the Tsar continued to trust the "arcanist".

In 1579 Ivan the Terrible ordered Bomelius to predict the future of his descendants. Hooked up in convulsions to the crystal ball, he began to predict that the second wife of the eldest son of the tsar would die in childbirth, Ivan IV personally would kill his own son. Sons Fedor and Dmitry will also die before their father. The Rurikovich family will be extinguished and there will be confusion. This caused the immediate wrath of the king and served as the beginning of the end of Bomelius's activities at court. Later Bomelius was accused of treason and burned alive in Moscow in 1580. This massacre made a very definite impression on foreigners at the court, because in his homeland Bomelius was also known as an evil man. For exactly the same charge, he was imprisoned in London. It is known that at the request of Ivan IV, to replace Bomelius, Elizabeth I in 1581 sent to Moscow a physician Robert Jacobi and pharmacist James Franch.

Another, authentic titan of mathematical sciences, cryptography, alchemy and astrology, Welshman John Dee was an adviser to several Royals. In Prague, where he lived for 3 years, he counseled the Emperor of the Holy Roman Empire, Rudolf II, who at that time had the reputation being King of the Alchemists. In England John Dee was renowned and even worked with the famous Italian Gerolamo Cardano (the inventor of the cardan shaft) in building the perpetual motion machine. The latter was unsuccessful, according to the judgment of the courtiers, made a horoscope to the 15-year-old King Edward VI, predicting a serious illness at the age of 55. However, the king died as a teenager, after which Cardano was disgraced. Edward's heir, Maria Tudor, entrusted the compilation of the horoscope to John Dee himself, which gained the trust of the Queen. There were rumors that he predicted the accession of Elizabeth and informed the princess about it in a letter that was intercepted by Maria's spies. Despite this, Dee managed to escape punishment. Relations with her successor, Elizabeth I, were even more successful for Dee. The coronation of Elizabeth on January 15 was appointed at the insistence of Dee. Under Elizabeth, Dee not only conducted scientific research, but also spying activities in other countries for the benefit of the English crown. His reports Dee signed "agent 007". This served as a prototype of the known fictitious character of James Bond from the author, spy and occultist Ian Fleming.

Just 4 years ago, the London Royal College of Physicians held an exhibition on January 18, 2014 "Scholar, courtier, magician: the lost library of John Dee" dedicated to the famous mathematician, astronomer, alchemist and occultist. One of the exhibits was the painting "John Dee conducts alchemical experiments before Queen Elizabeth I" by the artist of the Victorian era Henry Gillard Glindoni. When preparing the exhibition, the picture was examined in X-rays and unexpectedly appeared that the famous alchemist was originally depicted by the artist in a circle formed by human skulls. Curator of the exhibition Katie Birkwood believes that the artist painted over the skulls, as the customer of the painting considered them too gloomy for his taste.

Dee's talents were recognized in many European capitals. To Maria Tudor John Dee proposed to establish the Royal Library, which was to become the largest collection of scientific books in the modern world. When this project did not receive support, Dee began to collect his own library, which quickly turned into the richest private library in the country. A part of the books (3000) from the library of Dee he donated to the National Library. John Dee is also considered as the founder of the British Museum.

The interest of the Moscow court and the Tsar Fedor Ioannovich himself to alchemy and astrology was confirmed by an attempt in 1586 to invite to the service in Russia the mathematician, astrologer, alchemist and magician John Dee. Son of John, Arthur will later become a personal doctor and adviser to the Moscow Tsar Mikhail Romanov. At the request of Tsar Michail, King James I sent him to Russia. A study of the relevant sources clearly shows that he was chosen not so much by the English king but by Russian agents (who were sent to London to find a doctor "who was sufficiently knowledgeable and educated").

The archival record destroyed by the Moscow fire of 1812 mentioned "Messengers Yuri Rodionov and Andrei Kerkerlin, sent by Tsar Mikhail Feodorovich with a special secret mission to Germany, France and England, during their stay in England and Holland, with all certainty found that Dr. Arthur Dee " is very famous for his art ". Thus, Arthur Dee was widely known even before his arrival to Moscovia, and not only in London. Even before his departure, Arthur Dee was the court physician of King James I and Queen Anne, and this beside other things is confirmed by a document signed by Charles I, where Arthur Dee was called "the faithful doctor of King James." Perhaps, after listening to

Russian envoys, the king sent Arthur Dee to Moscow "at the special request of the Tsar." Simultaneously, James sent a letter to Tsar Michail in Moscow, in which he recommended Arthur Dee as a skilled doctor. The letter was dated 21 .06 1621. At the Moscow court, Artur Dee was known as Artem Ivanovich Diy. After 14 years of faithful service to Romanov, Artur Di returned to his homeland, where he became a personal physician and advisor to King Charles I.

The last imperial couple of the Russian Empire was also not alien to occultism. In addition to constant fascination with various kinds of "holy fools" and "prophets", who at various times exerted enormous influence on Nicholas II and Empress Alexandra Feodorovna, even more serious occultists were present at the court. French doctor-quack Philippe Anthelm Nizier from Lyon was one of the first occultists to manipulate the royal couple. Expelled from Lyon's medical school for some "sensational drugs", repeatedly fined for practicing medicine without a license in France, "doctor" Philip began to practice "psychic currents" and "astral forces." Two Russian noblewomen, who were among his extensive clientele, introduced him to a Royal Russian couple. He was invited to live in Tsarskoe Selo , one of the royal residences. There he engaged in "scientific" activities: he improved the practice of hypnosis, predicting the future, reincarnation and necromancy. With the help of Philip Tsar Nicholas could "communicate" with the ghost of his father, Alexander III. In addition, he allegedly did other "miracles": he controlled the weather and became invisible.

Thanks to close relations with the tsar, the charlatan was awarded the title of doctor of medicine in Russia, and the French authorities had to recognize that, since the emperor personally petitioned for him.

Philippe claimed that he could determine the sex of the unborn child with the help of his occult practices, after which the Empress had a false pregnancy. By the spring of 1903, the head of the foreign agents of the police department, Petr Rachkovsky, prepared a report in which, on the basis of information obtained from Paris, the magician was accused of quackery. Even after all this, Nicholas refused to recognize the quackery of Nizier, blaming in libel "foreign agents of influence". However, the trust was lost, although Nizier was removed from the court with honors and money.

Apprentice of Nizier, Gerard Anaclet Vincent Encausse, known in history as Papus, made an even more dizzying career in Russia, having founded in St. Petersburg a secret Lodge of Martinists, whose members were the Tsar himself, many of his courtiers and famous painter Nikolai Roerich. In 1901 he came to Russia to establish a school of psychophysiology that did not exist even in France. Papus was a member of the Theosophical society of madam Helena Blavatsky. Papus was introduced to the court by the Grand Duke Nikolai Mikhailovich, with whom he had made friends in France. Despite the fact that Nikolai and Alexandra were struck by the abilities of Papus, he did not want to stay in Russia, arriving in the country again only in 1905, at the invitation of Tsar Nicholas. Then the occultist, while visiting Tsarskoe Selo, "summoned" the spirit of Alexander III, who advised the tsar to ruthlessly suppress the revolution.

The last time Papus visited Russia was in 1906, but corresponded with Nikolai and Alexandra at least until 1915. In one of the letters he warned the empress about the evil, committed by Gregory Rasputin, "the holy demon." Papus writes that, from the point of view of the Kabbalist, he is "a vessel like Pandora's box, in which all the evil, all the vices and filthy motives of the Russian people are concentrated." "It's worth it to crash this vessel, or its terrible contents will spread over Russia," he warned. Upon learning of the death of the occultist in 1916, Alexandra Feodorovna wrote to her husband at the front: "Papus died, which means we are doomed." Probably, it was after acquaintance with these two characters that the royal family made a personal emblem of the swastika, which was previously actively promoted by madam Helena Blavatsky and her Theosophical Society, which at the time of her death had 60,000 members around the world. Even on the wall of the Ipatiev House, where the royal family were executed by the Bolshevics, a swastika inscribed by the Empress was found on the wall.

Personal vehicle of tsar Nicolas II Delaunay-Belleville

Diary of the Empress Alexandra

Post card of the empress Alexandra

After that, the swastika was still wandering from the Provisional Government's banknotes to the early Bolshevik symbols.

"The Russian state military archive, created in 1920 for" collecting historical material on the combat activities of the Red Army, "marks its 80th anniversary. The "Authorities" columnist Yevgeny Zhirnov visited the exhibition devoted to this event and discovered that during the Civil War some Red Army men went on attack in leather bast shoes and with a swastika on their sleeves. "'Kommersant" newspaper dated 01.08.2000

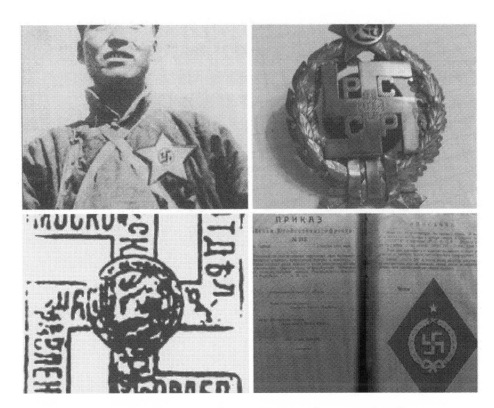

 Noteworthy is the occult activity of some high-ranking officials in the Cheka-NKVD (secret police and intelligence service, later KGB), in the early 20th to mid-1930s. Head of the Cryptographic Department (Special Department at the Cheka) Gleb Ivanovich Boky was a member of the secret occult organization "United Labor Brotherhood", studying the "Ancient Science of Dyunhor." Several times the sessions of the society were visited by Henry Jagoda himself - the future head of the NKVD.

Bokiy drew to the work of the Special Department in the winter of 1924 the learned mystic Alexander Barchenko. The main scientific interests of this researcher were concentrated in the field of studying the bioelectric phenomena of the cell, the work of the brain and in the living organism as a whole. His laboratory experiments Barchenko combined with the post of expert for Bokiy on psychology and parapsychology. In particular, he developed a technique for identifying individuals who are prone to cryptographic work and to decoding codes. The scientist acted as a consultant in the survey of all kinds of medicine men, shamans, mediums, hypnotists and other people who claimed that they had ability to communicate with ghosts. Since the late 1920s, the Special Department has actively used them in its work.

The research and methodology of Barchenko was also applied in particularly difficult cases of deciphering enemy messages - in such situations group sessions for the communication with spirits were conducted. To test these "psychics", one of the divisions of the service Bokiy's equipped a "black room" in the building of the OGPU (predecessor of NKVD) on Furkasovsky Lane, house N 1. Reports to Dzerzhinsky (head of secret police and intelligence service) were forwarded through the infamous agent Yakov Blumkin, who enjoyed the special access to Dzerzhinsky.

It is also known that the famous artist and Martinist Nikolai Roerich at one time enjoyed the patronage of Dzerzhinsky himself, who allocated for his expedition to Tibet, 600,000 dollars for the search for the mysterious Shambhala under the guise of Supreme Council of National Economy, which at that time was an enormous sum of money. Several members of the "United Labor Brotherhood" were included in the expedition. Despite the fact that Roerich was not even a Soviet citizen, Moscow asked the Mongolian Ministry of Foreign Affairs for a letter of protection for "Academician N.K. Roerich" with his wife and son for the right of unimpeded passage through Mongolian border to the Yum-Beise, not explaining neither the citizenship Roerich, nor the reason for the interest of the USSR in his diplomatic immunity, nor the final point of travel. Roerich had a great influence on his pupil, US Vice-President Henry Wallace, which further damaged latter's political career. During the presidential election of 1940, Republicans identified a series of letters written by Wallace to Nicholas Roerich. In these letters, Wallace addressed to Roerich as the "Dear Guru" and signed all his letters with the letter "G"

(Galahad). This name was given him by Roerich. Nicholas Roerich called himself the with Tibetan name of Ret Rigden. In these letters, Wallace wrote to Roerich that he was expecting "the coming of the New Day," when people from the Northern Shamballa set a beginning to the era of peace and prosperity. Wallace denied the authenticity of these letters.

Wallace was an adherent of Roerich and his ideas from the mid-1920s. With the consent of Roosevelt Wallace actively lobbied in the US Congress the "Roerich Pact" on the protection of art, scientific institutions and historical monuments, which was signed in Washington by delegates from 22 American countries in 1935. In 1934 The US Department of Agriculture sent Roerich with an expedition to search for drought-resistant plants to prevent the repetition of the Dust Bowl situation. The Dust Bowl, also known as the Dirty Thirties, was a period of severe dust storms that greatly damaged the ecology and agriculture of the American and Canadian prairies during the 1930s. However, during the expedition, Nicholas Roerich and his son Yuri conducted political activities, which politically compromised the US government, resulting in Wallace's early termination of the expedition. In his memoirs, he even made attempts to obscure his connections with Roerich and his spiritual teachings.

When in 1940 the Republicans threatened to publicize Wallace's occult beliefs, the Democrats responded by threatening to disclose information about Republican candidate Wendell Wilkie, who was rumored to have an extramarital relationship with writer Irita Van Doren. The Republicans agreed not to publish "letters of the Guru." However, in the winter of 1947 an independent columnist, Westbrook Pegler, published excerpts from these letters in the newspaper and used them in his articles as proof that Wallace is incompatible with the post of the president. In the elections of 1948, Wallace was a presidential candidate from the Progressive Party.

Some attribute to Nicholas Roerich the design of a one-dollar bill, known for its Masonic symbols, which he allegedly lobbied through Wallace. They claimed that the author of the design was a Russian emigre, Sergei Makronovsky, under whose pseudonym Roerich was supposedly hiding. It is not possible verify the veracity of this statement, but the connection between Roerich and Wallace and their passion for the occult is a historical fact.

By the end of the 1930s, most of the members of the secret Soviet, masonic and other occult organizations were either arrested or executed, such as a member of the Moscow Central Committee and Deputy Foreign Minister Stomonyakov, and Barchenko himself.

Although Joseph Stalin was not known for his fascination with the occult, but there is one episode in history, when he proved that he himself was not a stranger to superstition. There was an archaeological and anthropological expedition in June of 1941, as a result of which Tamerlane's(Timur) tomb was exhumed in Uzbekistan's Gur Emir. A lot of mystical details were circulating around this story, but the bare facts are, that despite the warning of the impending war by the three old men -local elders (with several alive witnesses) not to open the grave, the anthropological scientists A.Semenov, S. Aini, M.M. Gerasimov, T.N.Kari-Niyazov did not listen to the warning. As you know, the next day began Hitler's invasion of Soviet Union.

For a long time, scientists were arguing about the burial place of the great ruler of antiquity. The main "applicants" were the villages of Timur Kesh and Gur-Emir near Samarkand, where the remains of Tamerlan's son Shahrukh and grandson of Ulugbek were rested. It was decided to conduct excavations in Gur Emir. The Tamerlane's coffin was not opened immediately: the winch broke, the floodlights went out, the breathing inside the tomb became difficult. Involuntarily among the scientists started talk about the curse of Timur. In the pause between the works on the opening of the tomb, three old men approached operator Malik Kayumov and asked how the matter was progressing. The elders showed the operator a book in which it was written that if the Timur's coffin was to be opened, the great war would break out. Kayumov turned to his older comrades, but neither Ayni nor Semyonov, despite the chain of inexplicable phenomena, believed in the prophecy, although they also feared something, apparently knowing about the curse of the pharaohs and the fate of the archeologists who had opened the Ancient Egyptian tombs.

Later Malik Kayumov was appointed as cameraman for the Kalinin Front. In the spring of 1942 he met with a pre-war acquaintance, Lieutenant-General Porfiry Chanchibadze, and told him about the prediction of the elders. Chanchibadze told this to Fieldmarchall G.K Zhukov.

"And in the autumn of that year," recalls the cameraman, "Georgy Zhukov came to the front and it turned out that Chanchibadze told him about me, and a few days later Zhukov invited me to his dugout, where he asked me about those events in great detail. I asked where Timur's skull is now stored, I said that Gerasimov had taken him away, and then rumors were circulating that a plane with the remains of the Timurids was flying over the front line. "

Remains of Timur (Tamerlane) and his relatives (Shahrukh, Ulugbek, Muhammadsultan, Miranshakh) were buried in Samarkand on December 20, 1942. As if the Soviet troops expected only this, after a few days Stalingrad was liberated. Whether there were flights with remains over the front line simple rumors or so was it in fact, in any case the fact remains that Stalin believed that the remains should be returned to the burial place as soon as possible.

Philippine president, dictator Ferdinand Marcos and his wife Imelda Marcos believed in the power of the number 7 and the pyramid. I'm not sure if this is relevant, but President Marcos was born on September 11th (the fact that might have boosted his career). After his expulsion from the Philippines many miniature pyramids were found in his palace. The presidential yacht Ang Pangulo registration number 777. The length of the yacht was 77 meters. Originally the yacht was intended for the

Philippines as the part Japanese reparations after the occupation during the World War II. The yacht was received from Japan during the administration of President Carlos Garcia and had the original registration number 77. Under Marcos, the yacht was renamed twice, first The President (TP-777), then BRP Ang Pangulo. Several presidential cars had a license plate number 777. "Mrs. Marcos alights from a campaign van with license plate No. 777. The Marcoses are said to lay claim to 7 and 11, and people here listen when the numbers are discussed. The date the President chose for the elections was the e seventh of the month." - reported The New York Times 6.2.1986. However, all this did not help Marcos to win his last election, and the presidential couple was forced to flee to Hawaii, where Marcos ended his days. There was also a 777 Corporation, set up to hold stock for Mr. Marcos, who believes that his lucky number is 7, according to a former Marcos associate. (NYT 16.03.1986)

Presidential couple Marcos and Ronald Reagan during a visit to the United States in 1982

In order to slightly dispel the sensation of the complete unreality of the subsequent narrative, I will remind you that in history there has already been at least one US president who has subordinated his activities to occult beliefs. It was not so long ago, and this president was Ronald Reagan. It became clear only after his retirement. Journalists only knew that Nancy and Ronald Reagan have a kind of "friend" who helps them plan the president's schedule. Reporters, in particular correspondents of the Times magazine, tried to find out which "friend" they were talking about, but they did not succeed. The staff of the presidential administration only knew how to keep their mouths shut, otherwise they would quickly lose their posts. The secret was revealed in 1988, when the former White House chief of staff Donald Reagan wrote in his book "For the Record" that the "friend" of the presidential couple who managed to stay in the shadows for so long was in fact is an astrologer from San Francisco named Joan Quigley. "At one time I had a calendar on my desk," Regan said, "where every day was marked with a special ink color (green - favorable days, yellow - neutral, red - unfavorable) so that I remember when it is favorable to move the president of the United States from place to place, when planning his public appearances or starting negotiations with a foreign power. " After these words, many things fell into place. It became clear why Reagan's inauguration took place at 5 am, why the president's departure from the Andrews airbase was often assigned at the most uncomfortable time without the slightest need, and why he was postponing negotiations. We do not know if more powerful people stood behind the presidential couple than Joan Quigley but such information lifts to some degree a veil over the mechanisms of state power, which implies that our society is governed not only by the pragmatic or idealistic motives known to us.

CBS report of the president's astrologist Joan Quigley where she is only mentioned to be "astrologist of the First Lady"

However, one of the most interesting figures in power, apparently practicing occultism on his own is the current US president Donald Trump. Below you will find Trump's own hand acknowledgment of engaging in the ancient mystical teachings of Kabbalah on page 188 of his own book, "The Way Up", in the 2004 edition. As many people have already noticed during his speeches Tramp constantly shows with his hands the sign "666", which is widely known under the name of Okay sign. He shows it so often that people have already stopped paying attention. In addition, the Trump family lived on 66th floor of the Trump Tower in New York before moving to the White House. The height of the Trump Tower is 203 meters or 666 feet (curiously, $2/3 = 0.666$). His inheritance he received after the death of his grandmother Elizabeth Christ Tramp on 6.06.66(curious date as well). It is widely known from history, birth and death dates were frequently manipulated, in order to fit it into a beneficial combination of figures, as it probably happened when Pope John Paul II died the true date of his death was concealed to match his birth and passing with solar eclipses. Donald Trump's son-in-law Jared Kushner is the owner of the famous building 666 on Fifth Avenue. The building was purchased for 1.8 (6 + 6 + 6) billion dollars. Currently Kushner is busy, among other things, with the project of erecting a 666-foot skyscraper on the Journal square New Jersey for $ 666,000,000. Even if you will find such "coincidences" very strange, then you could verify them in search engines in the matter of seconds.

The president's son-in-law, Jared Kushner, and his building at 666 Fifth Avenue. At the moment 666 sign is removed from the upper part of the building

During the GOP primary 666 delegates for Tramp

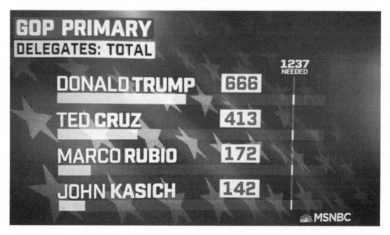

203 meters conversion to 666 feet (also 2/3=0,666)

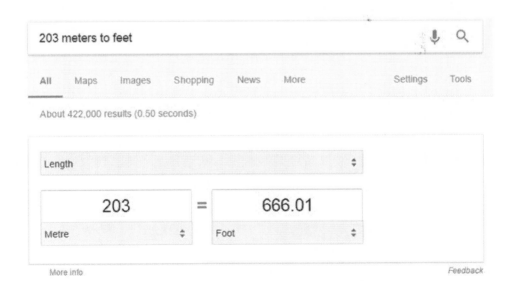

The commercial of Pizza Hut performed by Donald Trump personally where the pizza's price is coincidentally 9,99$ which is numerological hit to 666.

1995 Donald Trump Pizza Hut Commercial

Other Trump's Pizza Hut commercial with curious phone number designed according numerological principles (66 and 11 s)

Pizza Hut "New Yorker" TV ad (2000) featuring Donald Trump

Since the birth of Donald Trump before his inauguration as president of the United States has passed exactly 70 years, 7 months and 7 days. You can check it yourself by entering the date of his birth and the date of the inauguration in to the calculator. The list of "coincidences" can be continued indefinitely, but below I will try to explain their mechanism.

Just four years ago such a big official in the world financial system as the Executive Director of the International Monetary Fund Christine Lagarde in her speech to members of the Press club in Washington demonstrated not only her occult knowledge, but also made it clear to listeners, literally "I do that I was told ". She practically told the audience that she was just a performer. You can see for yourself by finding her speech on Youtube, as many media outlets have omitted this phrase in the transcript of her speech.

"Among many talents of the Executive Director of the International Monetary Fund, Christine Lagarde is gifted with metaphorical comparisons and a thorough knowledge of numerology.

It is these qualities Lagarde demonstrated on Wednesday in Washington to all gathered at the National Press Club, where she made economic forecasts for 2014 according to the version of the International Monetary Fund.

Lagarde firmly believes that setting the tone for 2014 will be the number 7, which is considered a sign of unconditional success and good luck. To reinforce her theory, Lagarde briefly reviewed the history, recalling that 2014 will be the hundredth anniversary of the end of the

First World War (the date plus the sum of the figures in the first anniversary), and the very sum of the figures in the date 2014(7).

It is noteworthy that in mentioning the "mystical sevens" important in the coming year, Lagarde referred to the "Big Seven" by neglecting or deliberately ignoring the transformation of the G-7 into the G-8, after Russia joined it, which, in addition to everything else, presides in this organization in the coming year.

"I hope that after seven terrible years for the economy, 2014 will open for us a seven-year economic success," said Christine Lagarde, moving from numerology to the content of her narrative. "

Reported by the channel VOA News.

I did not mention this, in order to prove that all higher state officials are prone to astrology, although, for example, in the countries of Southeast Asia and the Far

East, this is very common. The essence of what has been said is that there are forces in the world that are much more influential and little known than court astrologers of elderly fools at high positions. I will try to present to you the mechanisms of action of these forces in this book.

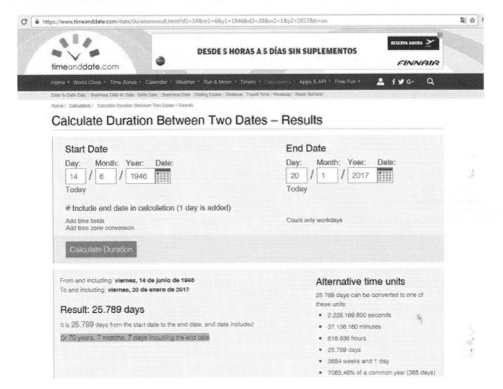

Chapter II Codes in Pop Culture and Media

For a long time in the circles of researchers was argued about what are in actuality these countless coincidences in hundreds of Hollywood films, cartoons, comic books, advertising and music videos? Within the thousands of units of such a production since the early 30s of the twentieth century, the crumbling twin towers were showing up, countless references to code 911 appeared (officially symbolizing in our time the events of September 11, 2001 in the USA). Some of the researchers explain this phenomena with the definition of the famous Swiss psychologist Karl Gustav Jung who coined the concept of synchronicity in the early 20th century. Synchronism is a coincidence that is so unusual and significant that it cannot be attributed exclusively to accidents. In a purely linguistic sense, synchronism is a mysterious phenomenon, when two or more events occur simultaneously, seemingly directly related to each other, although it would normally seem impossible. Others will explain this by a conspiracy among the elite, in which the famous Hollywood filmmakers could be the part of. Still others try to attribute all phenomena to the so-called apophenia- (from the Greek "I make a judgment," "I make it clear") - an experience consisting in the ability to see the structure and relationships in random or meaningless data. Someone is trying to give explanation of all this, saying that we are all inside the Matrix, a kind of simulated reality-concept, presented in the famous movie with Keanu Reeves in the title role.

Let's try to understand these hypotheses, taking for example one of the most cult films of our time, the trilogy "Back to the Future" directed by Robert Zemeckis, as well as several other related films.

Often even in the worst Hollywood "B" movies (where there are no big budgets and expensive actors), along with the main storyline, there is some occult subtext that the talented director realizes even within most unsuccessful plot. Some achieve both-great superficial storyline, great work of all actors, big budgets and intricate second story layers which are no less intelligent as the main storyline. Who are these Hollywood filmmakers and producers really that seem to be some kind of a close-knit sect, leaving their signs and rituals in their products? The overwhelming majority of them are Kabbalists and Freemasons, which in itself is not a big secret for anyone who is intently reading the chronicles or revolves in the close social circles. In some cases everything is much more serious, as in the case of the founder of one of the biggest studios in Hollywood Walt Disney. The great-great-grandfather of the famous creator of the studio, George Burroughs, was even hanged for witchcraft, as a result of the sensational trial of the Salem witches, at the end in 1692 -a fact that you can glean even from Wikipedia pages.

Wikipedia page, The Execution of George Burroughs, Walt Disney

Walt Disney is known for being co-opted by the predecessor of the CIA OSS for secret operations, performing secret missions in Europe during the World War II, sympathizing (mutually) to Adolf Hitler who revered his cartoon production.

Hitler's drawings of characters from Disney cartoons, discovered in 2008 dated 1940.

Disney's studio is also known for being repeatedly caught on the inserting of erotic images in the cartoons and films for children during decades.

Watchful spectators have found in Disney's cartoons naked bodies in the background, erect penises of cartoon characters and other unpleasantries. Sometimes, between the towers of fairy-tale castles the penises were found, and in the sky - the inscription of the word "sex", the ropes or belts bizarrely formed into this word ''sex'. Sometimes, the outlines of the silhouettes could be taken for the anatomical parts of the naked bodies. All this was not a product of the imagination of the overly vigilant viewers. Such images were based on the principles of marketing, the so-called 25th frame, only in the case of Disney studio work, it was not only about trying to subliminally sell a certain product to prospective buyers in the future, the current kids, but an attempt at sexual corruption from an early age. However, all this is so vast of the theme, which in itself can be the subject for a separate book. Here this topic will be touched only casually, to outline the context in which the "mages" of the twentieth and twenty-first centuries operate.

Fragments and photos from Disney cartoons with erotic overtones: Footage from Disney's "Little Mermaid" before and after editing, screenshots from the cartoon "The Lion King" with erotic overtones, "Rapunzel, tangled story":

To begin with, I need to make clear that you'd need to be familiar with the basic rules of numerology, in order to correctly read codes in movies, articles, Internet portals, etc. Rule number one, from the change of places of digits meaning and the value of the number does not change. For example, the code 911, which was implemented on September 11, 2001, and was designated as 911, at first glance only by date in the media, can be manifested as follows: 911, 119, 116, 191,161, 611, or even more subtle, when for example the date of publication of a material in a newspaper or on an Internet portal, the dates of the release of a movie could be obtained by simply adding up several figures to manifest desired code. Another widely used way to designate the code long before September 11, 2001 was the display of the twin towers of the New York City's WTC, in combination with an airplane flying over or near them, or simply destroying them with an explosion. The result, however, should symbolize the same sacred figure 911.

Rule number two: 9 and 6 are interchangeable. Remember the famous song of Jimi Hendrix "If 6 was 9 ". What is remarkable, the song was released in 19**69**. Pay attention to the very combination of numbers. By the way, it was Jimi Hendricks who said in an interview with Life magazine in 1969:

"The atmosphere is created, because music, in fact, is a spiritual thing ... you can hypnotize people ... and when you find them at the most sensitive moment, you can subconsciously preach what you want to say." (Life, October 3, 1969, p. 74)

Rule number 3: 0 has no value and is freely discarded when calculating.

All of the above, does not mean that the author of these lines unreservedly believes in numerology. I give her great importance, since from the times of ancient mysticism, as in our time, numerology is still used in various spheres of life every day. For correct interpretation of secret codes in modern media and Hollywood products, one must be familiar with numerology, in the same way as a person who tries to learn an unfamiliar foreign culture should begin with learning a foreign language. Presently the author was able to identify a dozen basic codes, of which less than half were deciphered. Existence of these codes in the media and pop culture is undeniable due to hundreds of revealed examples that cannot be attributed to pure coincidence. However, the significance of these codes is far from obvious, although it is always possible to identify some constant patterns of usage. A striking example is code 322, which is the official code of the secret brotherhood of Skull and Bones from the Yale University in the United States. Members of this secret society are many well-known politicians and businessmen, both ex-US President George Herbert Walker Bush and George Bush Jr., President Taft, former US Secretary of State John Kerry and many other famous, influential people. In all official photographs of members Skull and Bones (which are available mostly until 1960s), number 322 is clearly visible beneath skull and crossed bones, the meaning of which none of its members has the right to disclose. According to the semi-official version, 322 has something to do with Demosthenes, but this should not be taken too seriously. So-far I have not cited all the widely used codes in order not to deal with the explanations of those codes, the existence of which, for the most of the readers is still not obvious. In order to make these facts evident enough for uninitiated reader I intend to give some obvious examples and only after that attempt to interpret them.

If you will find ridiculous the very suggestion of looking codes in the media, films and other elements of pop culture, then I recommend checking the covers of the most prestigious British magazine The Economist, owned by the Rothschilds at least ones a year. Every year the magazine offers the readers a charade on its front cover depicting world's leaders, political and economic events in a cryptic form. It is titled "World in 2016", "2017", "2018" and so on. Chairman of the media holding The Economist Group is Lin Forester de Rothschild, wife of Sir Evelyn Robert de Rothschild. No correct answers are ever offered to the readers even at the end of the year. Some events though will transpire at the later stage proving that the charade was no matter of mere entertainment.

Chapter III Back to the Future and Code 911

Let us revisit "Back to the Future" (1985) and its director Robert Zemeckis: In the first part of the film there is a scene of attack by Middle Eastern terrorists at the parking lot of the Trade Center "Twin Pines" (an obvious reference to the twins towers of the New York City World Trade Center, which will be destroyed by real Middle Eastern terrorists 16 years later, at least so it says the official version. The time of the attack is 1:16 am, which turns into 9:11 (if viewed upside down).

Screenshot of terrorist attack:

After the terrorist attack, the Twin pine mall turns into a Lone pine mall symbolizing the Freedom Tower (World Trade Center of the One World), built on the site of the fallen twin towers in 2011, in New York.

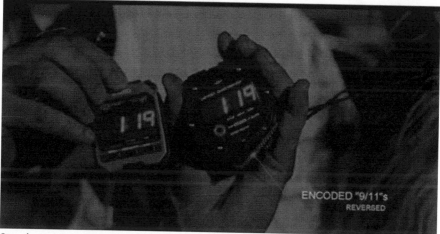

Synchronizing stopwatches with 1:19(911)

In the second part of the trilogy twin pines appearing again

Twin towers displayed in the window and then they are crumbling due to the "broken window"

Next in front of the screen appears the torch of the Statue of Liberty, which in fact, 16 years later, "looked" upon crumbling towers.

View of a room with a torch of the Statue of Liberty

Real view in NYC

One of the Mc Flays family hangs upside down in the room in front of the towers on the screen, so when they disappear from the screen, they just crumble as happened in real live on 11/9/01.

Thus, the terrorist attack of September 11, 2001 (911) by Arab terrorists was not only "predicted" in the film but also embellished with a warning about it, that Marty tried to warn about "Doc" Brown. According to the plot he dies in the future by the hands of those terrorists. Screenshot of Marty trying to shout to Doc Brown a warning, then tries to write him a letter.

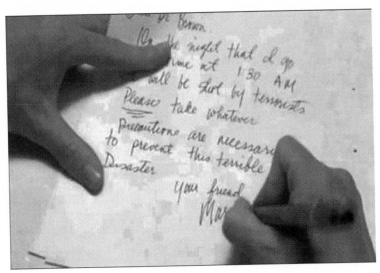

Burning tire marks and 9 in the left upper part of the screen form 911. Pay attention to the burning wire across the screen. The clock shoes time 10:04

Dashboard inside of the time machine

In real life in October of 2015 director Robert Zemeckis releases another blockbuster (30 years later "Back to the Future") "The Walk" which describes the incredible fit of French tight wire walker Philip Petit

The wire is prominent in both movies and not accidental

Doc Brown attaches the wire to the clock tower

The wire and clock with 10:04, with the help of the lightning transfers the protagonists to the future

30 years between both movies but both protagonists are dressed, cut and basically look the same

Thus, incredibly the famous filmmaker stretched out the wire in time throughout a whole 30 years, tied up the terrorist attack by the Arabs, 911 and the twin towers. What is it? Matrix? Conspiracy? A string of incredible coincidences? Let's try to deal with this in more detail considering a few more codes that appear in this cult film.

CHAPTER IV CODE 88

Equally important for the film is code 88 which runs through the entire trilogy. When the speed 88 miles per hour was reached by Delorian DCM 12, which served to the protagonists as a time machine, it started its journey through epochs and spaces.

The story of discovering this little- known code is curious. About 5 years ago a few newspaper articles from the international media attracted my attention. Then, in 2012, it was reported the discovery of several grand concert pianos in Florida lonely standing at the beach. It would seem, that these strange, but not very remarkable discoveries should not have been on the pages of the international press, but nevertheless they got there. What is the connection between grand pianos and 88? It is quite simple the standard concert piano has 88 keys.

As it probably quite clear to everyone, the grand concert piano, in whatever technical condition is a fairly expensive thing. No one in their right mind will throw away such a piano, dragging it secretly to the beach. Even a particularly advanced artist-installer will not undertake such a "performance" without claiming his authorship. All these grand pianos remained anonymous and were not even instantly removed by the municipal authorities as an unattended garbage. After some time in the media might appear short articles hinting on "a student's prank," or something like that. Nevertheless, if it was only the matter of slightest suspicion of prank the news agencies would not spread such a dubious news without a certain, pre-conceived goal.

Northwest Florida Daily News shared Devon Ravine's photo.

April 2, 2013 · 🌐

MYSTERY PIANO SHOWS UP ON ISLAND

Then there were reports of open-air concerts in New York with 88 concert grand pianos. Quite strange idea for manifestation of the code although more logical one. Similar concerts for the 88 pianos were held in other countries of the world. Below is one more episode from 2013 with 88 pianos placed in different areas of New York. The organizers of the concert called on the participants:

" Do you like playing the piano on the fresh air? ' Then you come to New York! Thus, the long-awaited project "Sing for Hope" was launched. In 5 districts of the city 88 grand concert pianos were installed. As expected, thousands of fingers will run through these keys during the project. "

According to the organizers of such concerts, the idea appeared "spontaneously" and began to turn into a tradition.

The Manila Symphony Orchestra celebrates its 88th anniversary. The concert opens with 88 Symphony by Haydn in B major ". So far so good, strange but really weird enough to suspect something more serious.

Further it will get weirder though this comes from much earlier times: According to the New York Times the highest daily temperature on August 8, 1988 in New York City, believe it or not, reached 88 degrees Fahrenheit. Another manipulation of numbers in the media or a rare genuine coincidence? In general, this article in NY Times is very remarkable by itself. It will not be understood not only by the average American, but even by a fairly educated New Yorker. In the frivolous, only by insiders alone, understandable manner, the article hints at some sort of numerological importance of the number 88. It would probably seem to the average New Yorker only a combination of a satire and gossip column in one. However, everything was calculated, probably, those in the know would understand the true meaning.

''Acht! It's the eighth day of the eighth month of the eighty-eighth year of this enervating century, but you're far too slow. The number 8888 sold out faster than any other in the history of the New York State Lottery's Win Four game, all 1,000 tickets gone by 11:37 A.M. on Aug. 1, the first day they were offered.

"It went like flash paper," said Russell Gladieux, acting director of the lottery. The odds are 1 in 10,000 that 8888 will be drawn shortly before 8 tonight.

The odds on the temperature rising above 88 degrees, however, are judged pretty good. In The New York Times of Aug. 8, 1888, the weather is described as "Still Warm and Moist," which might also define the prose. "Promise of a respite from hot weather was not fulfilled," the paper said. "For by noon the sun was uncovered and cast its burning rays on the city. At that hour, even where shade protected the mercury, the thermometer indicated 76 degrees, and was still on the ascendant."

Mercury is a sort of motif here. While numerologists, who study the occult significance of numbers, disagree about what the day holds, most seem to concur that the number 8 represents the planet Mercury, named after the divinity of messenger boys and commerce, and thus a favorite of ad agencies. A few numerologists plump for Uranus, but somebody should.

Eight is considered a particularly amusing sort of number by the American Mathematical Society, which marks its centennial today in Providence, R.I.

Eight is the second cube, the sixth Fibonacci number, the sum of the first three digits of pi and the largest number, because it is infinity turned on its head. Or on its tail. Or perhaps its side. Coupled with V, eight becomes a powerful totem of the American road. Vegetarians, however, think V8 is a drink.

Numerologists say eight is the number of business executives, administrators and other assorted materialists, who are cold and clever and thus perhaps a bit preoccupied to make very attentive partners, at least in love.

Kristina Volpech, a Los Angeles numerologist, is of the commercial school. "As for the business world, it should be an exceptionally powerful day," she said.

Sue Schachter clearly has heard this quiet call of the cosmos. Ms. Schachter, whose press representatives describe her as "top agent to children and sports personalities," has decided to publicize her 49th birthday today. According to Canaan Communications Inc., Ms. Schachter will have a party, beginning at 8 P.M., at "the legendary steakhouse, Kenny's," at Lexington Avenue and 50th Street. Venus Rules Today

"Celebrities and psychics expected to attend" include: Shirley MacLaine's psychic, Nancy Reagan's astrologer, Christopher Reeve, John McEnroe and Tatum O'Neal, Jackie Mason and Jerry Rubin. Some people will go to anything. Why shouldn't you? If you're not a recognized celebrity, perhaps you're a psychic. Who's to know?

Rock Kenyon, who says he's a psychic as well as a numerologist, thinks playing the markets might be a bad idea today. Using the Fadic system -which reduces every collection of numbers to a single digit - Mr. Kenyon conjures 8/8/1988 to yield six, and thus predicts a day ruled by Venus, the planet of love, sex and illusion.

"It's not a great day for investing," Mr. Kenyon insisted. "Stay home and make love." Those seeking any further guidance on this conundrum will note that on Aug. 8, 1888, the Dow Jones average rose 2.8 points, to 85.97, a new high for that tumultuous year, during which Jack the Ripper stalked London; Edward Bellamy published "Looking Backward", and the Parker Pen Company was established at Janesville, Wis.

No Partying Planned 8/8/88 was inauspicious, however, for the Spanish Armada, which lost its last ship on this day 400 years ago.

At 888 Eighth Avenue in Manhattan, Senator Bill Bradley found love and marriage, meeting his wife-to-be, Ernestine Schlant, a professor of German language and literature. For some reason, best unexamined, this was remembered by an office savant, or psychic, and confirmed yesterday by Senator Bradley's good-natured press secretary, Nick ("You can't have a Bill and be a Nicholas") Donatiello.

But the doorman of 888 Eighth Avenue, Jose Diaz, said yesterday that no party was planned for today. "Nobody's having a party - this is an apartment building," Mr. Diaz said. A Similar Celebration

This is a poor P.R. performance compared to July 7, 1977, when the Taft Hotel, at 777 Seventh Avenue, celebrated with prizes every seven minutes and a Dance of the Seven Veils. NYT 8.08.88

In Mandarin, noted R.L. Graham of AT&T Bell Laboratories, ba means both eight and father. Put the eighth day together with the eighth month and you've got Father's Day, at least in Taiwan.

"If seven is the number of perfection," said Rabbi Shalom Carmy, a professor of Jewish studies and philosophy at Yeshiva University, "then eight is the number that's one step beyond perfection."

His colleague at Yeshiva, Rabbi Dr. Moses Tendler, professor of Talmudic law, said: "The number seven, since it represents the seventh day of creation, is natural law. Eight is supranatural. For that reason circumcision occurs on the eighth day." So now you know. Not to tempt fate, gremlins willing, this compendium contains 888 words. But that's only if you believe, with Venus, that hyphens create something singular."

How about that? -"88 year old Yogi Berra moved in to this house in 1974."

www.princegeorgecitizen.com/sports/baseball/yogi-berra-s-new-jersey-home-for-sale-for-888-000-hall-of-famer-lived-

Yogi Berra's New Jersey home for sale for $888,000; Hall of Famer lived there almost 40 years

THE ASSOCIATED PRESS
MAY 2, 2014 08:00 PM

The house where former New York Yankees player Yogi Berra lived for 40 years is seen, Friday, May 2, 2014, in Montclair, N.J. The six-bedroom, 3½-bathroom colonial is for sale for $888,000. The baseball Hall of Famer wore No. 8 on his jersey when he played for the New York Yankees. The 88-year-old and his wife moved into the house in 1974. (AP Photo/Julio Cortez)

October 26 (88, 2+6, October from Greek "octo"-8, 8th month of Roman calendar) 1944 reported the death of 88 year princes Beatrice which was born in 1888 though the Wikipedia gives different date.

The Evening Independent - Oct 26, 1944   Browse this newspaper »   Browse all newspapers »

Princess Beatrice Succumbs at 88

London, Oct. 26—Æ—Princess Beatrice, youngest and last surviving child of Britain's famed Queen Victoria and mother of former Queen Victoria Eugenie of Spain, died today.

She was a great aunt to King George and the Duke of Windsor, and her family ties reached into many of Europe's royal families, some now deposed. She died at 5:10 a. m.

An official bulletin said Princess Beatrice died peacefully in her sleep. She would have been 88 next April 14.

Former Queen Victoria Eugenie came from Switzerland by air to be at her mother's side. A son, the Marquis of Carisbrooke, also

duties being discharged by a deputy coroner.

Princess Beatrice spent much of each year in Carisbrooke castle. She was an enthusiastic autograph collector, her albums containing the signatures of most European rulers and celebrities of the past 50 years. She also collected phonograph records of classical music, and was noted for her paintings.

She was married to Prince Henry in 1888 on the Isle of Wight in a church her father had designed and rebuilt by Queen Victoria. Prince Henry died of fever aboard a British warship off the African coast after taking part in the Ashanti campaign of 1895.

FINE COFFEE
FRESHLY ROASTED

Colonial Blend	lb. 36c
Supreme Blend	lb. 42c
Home Blend	lb. 30c

Fahrenheit 88

Directions

Fahrenheit 88 is a shopping mall located in the Bukit Bintang shopping district of Kuala Lumpur, Malaysia. The Fahrenheit 88 building reopened in August 2010 after undergoing extensive renovation works. Wikipedia

Address: 179 Jalan Bukit Bintang, 55100 Kuala Lumpur, Wilayah Persekutuan Kuala Lumpur, Malaysia

Opened: August 8, 2010

Hours: Closing soon · 10:00 am – 10:00 pm

Reviews

3.7 ★★★★★ 17 Google reviews

In March of 2014 in New York, multi-apartment building located above the store "Absolute Piano", blew up from the supposed gas explosion that caused a fire in the entire building. The main hero of the story was a certain Colin

Patterson, an employee of a store (Absolute piano) that sold these musical instruments, miraculously escaped death in the explosion. He was saved because the "cluster of pianos" softened the blow of the blast wave. So describes the incident channel Fox News. Immediately draws attention the address of the incident-116 street (code 911), which here stands next to the code 88. Also suspicious that there were few 44 old victims for 44 is 88/2 and also widely used part of the 88 code in the movies and mass media.

"EAST HARLEM -- Federal investigators are on the scene of an explosion and two building collapses at **116th Street** and Park Avenue in East Harlem, while rescue crews search for those still missing.

The explosion happened at either 1644 or 1646 Park Avenue around 9:30 a.m.

Both buildings collapsed down to the first floor, littering the area with debris

At least eight people are dead and 70 others injured, at least two of them critically

Rescue workers are searching for any other victims, with several occupants of the buildings still unaccounted for

A team of NTSB experts has arrived to investigate the cause of the explosion

One of the victims was identified as 44-year-old Griselde Camacho, a public safety sergeant at Hunter College. The second victim was identified as 67-year-old Carmen Tanco, who lived on the second floor of one of the buildings.

Rosaura Hernandez-Barrios, 21, was killed. In addition, Andreas Panagopoulos, 42, Alexis Salas, 22, Rosaura Barrios, 44, George Amadeo, 44 were identified on Thursday.

At least 70 other people are injured, at least two of them critically, including a 15-year-old boy. Harlem Hospital reports it has 13 patients, and Mount Sinai received 26 patients, including three children.

Metropolitan Hospital has 18 patients, and New York Presbyterian-Weill Cornell Medical Center has at least two. At least 27 people were treated and released." -Reports ABC.

SEARCH

NEW YORK POST

> to
be
>...

EPA chief says his
next flight will be
coach

NYC-to-Hamptons
helicopter service
partners with Airbus

Explosion survivor saved by 'cocoon' of pianos

By Reuven Fenton, Kenneth Garger and Laura Italiano   March 12, 2014 | 6:36pm

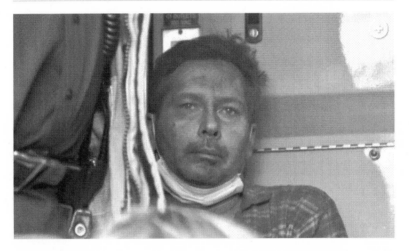

Meanwhile the survivor, the employee of Absolute **Piano** store was interviewed by the local television channel WCBS **88**0, affiliated with CBS. Quite a coincidence? Remember that 0 has no value in numerology and therefore is not taken into account.

All these strange coincidences made me take a closer look at the appearance of 88 in the media and films.
Immediately a very strange story emerged reported by the leading American media outlets 8.08. 2012. It was reported that fire was detected on the 88th floor of the Freedom

Tower (the new One World WTC, built on the site of the destroyed Twin Towers in NY). Allegedly firefighters were called after the appearance of smoke in one of the offices located on the **88**th floor of the Freedom Tower on **8.8**.12. A few days later, the veracity of this story was refuted by the same media, which by itself seemed strange, since such information is usually obtained by the media not from onlookers, but from the press centers of the New York Police and Fire Departments. Anyway, the main purpose of these reports was not to cover a real event, but to mention on the 8th day of the 8th month the fire on the 88th floor in a sacred place-the Ground Zero. The fire was described by the media as follows:

''Firefighters responded to an apparently false alarm on the 88th floor of the under-construction 1 World Trade Center tower Wednesday morning. Port Authority spokesman Steve Coleman said the fire report was called in by a member of the public. The civilian may have seen sparks from welding on the tower. About 84 firefighters responded to the 7:42 a.m. incident. No injuries were reported.''Ney York Daily News 8.08.12

DAILY●NEWS | NEW YORK

NYC Crime   Bronx   Brooklyn   Manhattan   Queens   Education   Weather

False alarm! Fire scare on 88th floor of 1 Center

Christian Science Monitor tells a little more:

Fire at 1 World Trade Center: maybe yes, maybe no. Confused?

The New York Fire Department and the owner of 1 World Trade Center give conflicting accounts of a report of fire Wednesday at the building, which is under construction at the site of the 9/11 attacks.

By Ron Scherer, Staff writer AUGUST 8, 2012

Andrew Burton/Reuters

NEW YORK — After 90 firefighters showed up at 1 World Trade Center early Wednesday, reports circulated of a fire on the 88th floor. In flash, camera crews arrived at the site of the

9/11 attacks. Journalists started writing stories that quickly got picked up by Google News and other news aggregators.

The only problem: There was no fire, at least according to the owner of the building, which was topped off on at an informal ceremony last Thursday when a steel beam signed by President Obama was erected on the 104th floor.

"The FDNY searched the building and found nothing," says Steve Coleman, a spokesman for the Port Authority of New York and New Jersey, which owns and is developing the site. "My construction guys are telling me there never was any fire."

So, why did 90 New York City firefighters show up at the site?

"I guess there was a report," says Mr. Coleman, "but they checked it out and they found no fire."

Well, not quite, says the New York Fire Department press office.

FDNY says it received a call about a fire at 7:42 a.m.

"There seemed to be a fire in the welding operation," says a spokesman for the department. The first was under control by 8:38 a.m., the department says.

Told that the Port Authority denies there ever was a fire, the press officer replied, "Wait for the fire marshall to investigate. It is definitely under investigation – call back later."

Coleman was not available for a follow up. He was in a meeting with Port Authority officials, trying to figure out what happened.

After construction of the building is complete in 2014, the tower will reach **1,776(888x2)** feet, counting the antenna on the roof. The building, which was once called the Freedom Tower, is still being leased out to future occupants. Conde Nast, the publisher, will be a major tenant, leasing more than 1 million square feet of space.

This real or fictitious fire reminded of a different story related to twin towers, which relates directly to the events of September 11, 2001. There is a documentary about the heroism of New York firefighters on the 88th floor, of burning WTC during 911. The documentary is titled "Heroes of the 88th floor."

''Special shows how the bravery of two men in the World Trade Center's North Tower changed the lives of countless people on 9/11. Through interviews with survivors, archival footage, and recreations, viewers will learn how construction manager Frank De Martini and construction inspector Pablo Ortiz saved **77** people on the tower's **88**th floor and inspired others to do the same.'' Describes the documentary IMDB.

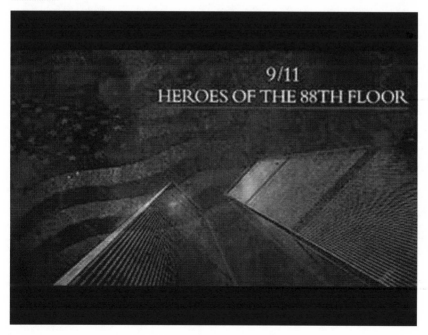

There is other direct link between Ground Zero-Twin Towers, today's Freedom tower and code 88-so called Tribute in Light. An art installation of **88** searchlights placed six blocks south of the World Trade Center to create two vertical columns of light to represent the Twin Towers in remembrance of the September 11 attacks. It is produced annually by the Municipal Art Society of New York.

The two beams cost approximately $1,626 (assuming $0.11 per kWh) to run for 24 hours. There are 88 xenon spotlights (**44 for each tower**) which each consume 7,000 watts. Wikipedia   Coincidentally April 4th, 1973 is official day of WTC opening. April 4th is a date with numerology of 44, April being the 4th month and it being on the 4th day (44).

The Petronas Twin Towers in Malaysia, not only have 88 floors, postal code containing 88, telephone number 88, but 88,000 glass and steel panels. Each of the towers is basically 8 in cross-section, with 8 corners and 8 rounds. The beams are purple. Purple=88 (8×11) in simple gematria.

purple = 16+21+18+16+12+5 = 88 (Ordinal)

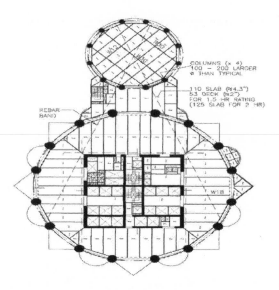

All these very strange coincidences made me take a more closer look at media reports, as well as pop culture events, especially around the topic of terrorism, September 11, movies about time travel, like "Back to the Future" to study if there is a link between the codes 911 and 88, which hasn't been found out previously. After couple of years of research, events began to develop with dizzying speed, when a whole layer of information was revealed. It all started with the trilogy "Back to the Future", and full circle 5 years later, making me look at the code 88 in a completely different light. I must point out that the surface value of the code 88 as the neo-Nazi greeting "Heil Hitler", is widely known among the skinheads. Letter H in English alphabet has the 8th ordinal number. Similarly, among the same neo Nazis and white supremacists, 18 stands for the initials of Adolf Hitler (A-1th letter and H-8th s letter of the English alphabet). However, this category of "conspirators" is very unimportant and marginal, therefore such an interpretation of the code would be considered naive for other, more large-scale events. By the way, this topic is not forbidden even in German and Russian media, and this interpretation of the code 88 has repeatedly appeared in respective media. These countries have most rigid laws against usage of the Nazi symbols anywhere. For example, several years ago, there was a scandal related to the Ariel wash powder brand belonging to the chemical conglomerate Proctor and Gamble. After vigilant journalists discovered large numbers 18 and 88 on various packages with washing powder, in May 2014 Proctor and Gamble was forced to remove these packages from the sale. British Daily Mail reported about this on May 10th 2014, though in a quite frivolous manner:

''Aryan automatic! Detergent giant caught up in Nazi row after Ariel boxes feature secret far-right code in Germany

Packages printed with large number '88', used by extremists for 'Heil Hitler'

Germany bans Nazi slogans, symbol used as His 8th letter of alphabet

Company forced to apologize after outraged shoppers took to Twitter

Also forced to pull 'Ariel 18' liquid as '18' is symbol for 'AH' or Adolf Hitler

Ariel detergent has sparked outrage in Germany after placing a neo-Nazi code on a new line of promotional packages.

The boxes feature a white football shirt with a large number '88' - which far-right extremists use as a code for 'Heil Hitler' to skirt the country's ban on Nazi slogans.

The number was intended to show how many loads of laundry buyers would be able to do with one package.

The number 88 is used by neo-Nazis to represent 'Heil Hitler' as Germany has a ban on Nazi slogans   +

Controversy: The number 88 is used by neo-Nazis to represent 'Heil Hitler' as Germany has a ban on Nazi slogans   +3

Controversy: '88' is used by neo-Nazis to represent 'Heil Hitler' as Germany has a ban on Nazi slogans

However, it is common knowledge in Germany that neo-Nazis have given the number a new meaning. The symbol derives from that fact that 'H' is the eighth letter of the alphabet.

Mother of neo-Nazi teen compared him to Sandy Hook school...

The idea even the Nazis called 'genius' that made D-Day...''

The brand's parent company, Procter & Gamble, has issued an apology for 'any false connotations' after shoppers took to Twitter posting pictures of the offending powder.

The firm yesterday acknowledged that the number was 'unintentionally ambiguous.'

Ariel 18 liquid detergent has also been pulled from German shelves as '18' represents 'AH', or 'Adolf Hitler'

'We very much regret if there are any false associations and distance ourselves clearly from any far-right ideology,' company spokeswoman Gabi Hassig said in a statement.

Haessig said the company has stopped shipping the offending powder.

They have also pulled a liquid detergent that was being promoted as 'Ariel 18' - which represents 'AH', as in Adolf Hitler.

Similar story was broken by the Russian local media in city of Yekaterinburg:

"Bank deposit Hitler"

In Yekaterinburg just shortly before the Victory Day (commemoration of the Victory over Nazi Germany in 1945), a Nazi scandal broke out

On the eve of May 9, a neo-Nazi scandal erupted in Yekaterinburg. One of the largest banks in the Urals has launched an advertising campaign, promising pensioners a deposit of 14.88% per annum. The erudite townspeople saw an encrypted Nazi salute and raised a wave of public protest. A scandal erupted in Yekaterinburg on the eve of Victory Day.

Bank "Jewels of the Urals" Universal bank has been active in the financial market of the Ural region since 1990.

Dozens of billboards of the bank "Jewels of the Urals" appeared in many cities of the Sverdlovsk region in mid-April. Within the framework of the advertising campaign, which many banks begin before large national holidays, potential investors were offered to make deposits on special terms. The bank, which positions itself as a family bank, offered to invest money at 14.88% per year. However, on their website, the placement conditions were somewhat different from those claimed on street boards. The interest rate was specified in the range of 11.5% - 13.5%, and the deposit could be made not only by veterans, but also by all who had fifteen hundred rubles.

The number of 14.88% was shown only on street advertising media, where it was indicated that such a high rate was calculated from the capitalization of interest."

Of course, bank officials were trying to downplay the meaning of the incident stating that 14,88% interest rate was calculated naturally from the pertinent data.

It was the end of 2015, when Donald Trump's election campaign was in full swing, large amount of interesting information about candidates for the US presidency being thrown into the media space. Leading information agencies of the world, including Russian TASS, quoted the interview of the author of the script for the "Back to the Future" trilogy Bob Gale. In this interview to Internet portal The Daily Beast Gale said that the image of Biff Tannen in the alternative reality of the film was conceived from the personality of Donald Trump. This similarity was traced not only to the mannerism of Biff, but also in portrait resemblance to his prototype. Moreover, the Pleasure Paradise Hotel and Casino from the film served as a parody of the famous Trump Tower.

"Back to the Future writer: bad guy Biff was based on Donald Trump"

Screenwriter Bob Gale confirms long-standing fan theory that Marty's nemesis in the trilogy was modelled on the Republican presidential candidate

'We thought about it when we made the movie' ... Back to the Future screenwriter Bob Gale on Biff's resemblance to Donald Trump.

'We thought about it when we made the movie' ... Back to the Future screenwriter Bob Gale on Biff's resemblance to Donald Trump. Photograph: YouTube

Back to the Future writer Bob Gale has revealed that the trilogy's villain Biff Tannen is based on Donald Trump, putting an end to fan speculation.

In the second film, which was celebrated this week as part of Back to the Future day, Tannen becomes a successful businessman who opens a 27-story casino and, in an oddly prescient touch, uses his money to influence US politics.

"We thought about it when we made the movie! Are you kidding?" Gale said to the Daily Beast. "You watch Part II again and there's a scene where Marty confronts Biff in his office and there's a huge portrait of Biff on the wall behind Biff, and there's one moment where Biff kind of stands up

and he takes exactly the same pose as the portrait? Yeah."
Reported British Guardian October 25th 2015

In addition, the action in the alternative reality of the film
unfolded in October of the same year 2015, which was
intended to draw special attention to it. For example, in
one of the episodes of the alternative year 2015, Marty is

in front of the building Pleasure Paradise Hotel and Casino, where amidst the ruins, mountains of garbage, general poverty, the lights of the casino Biff Tannen's were shining in dissonance. A gang of bikers approaches the building, and the sign reads "Welcome bikers!"

During the presidential campaign of Donald Trump bikers played an important role in the US media space, organizing numerous rallies in support of his candidacy.

Bikers for Trump in Florida heading out to Washington DC for the Inauguration.

Pay attention to the address of guy which speaks to Marty from TV screen in the alternate reality of BTF. "**88** Oriole road"

Soon Marty gets fired. He receives the fax message which reads "You are fired!" That very phrase later will be used by Donald Trump in show "The Apprentice".

Chapter V Gematria

Before I will clearly demonstrate the connection between Trump and code 88, I must make a digression, which is intended to clarify the way to encrypt the required numbers in to the texts, that it would not seem too obvious. This ancient numerological practice is called gematria. Gematria is one of the methods of analyzing the meaning of words and phrases based on the numerical values of the letters included in them. There are about a dozen of such systems, but the most commonly used ones are Jewish, Chaldean, English, Pythagorean(reduced) and simple(ordinal) gematria. Similar systems exist in Arabic abdjadiya, akshara-sankhya in Devanagari, Isopsephy in languages with Greek and Cyrillic script. The secret practice of encrypting and interpreting ciphers dates back to the Assyrian-Babylonian times and continues to be practiced today not only in Jewish mysticism (Kabbalah), but also among contemporary followers of the great alchemists of the XVI -XVIII centuries. The subject of the importance of gematria in Western European mysticism and alchemy deserves a separate study, but here we will touch this topic just superficially in order to show in practice how certain numbers are encoded into texts, being invisible to most of the readers. The most primitive method of simple gematria I mentioned above, describing the neo-Nazi greeting of HH, where the letters denote their digital order in the alphabet-8.

This code is based on the old English alphabet of 24 letters. It is well-known and its use has been documented well back into the medieval period.

Simple English Gematria Chart:

A=1	J=10	S=19
B=2	K=11	T=20
C=3	L=12	U=21
D=4	M=13	V=22
E=5	N=14	W=23
F=6	O=15	X=24
G=7	P=16	Y=25
H=8	Q=17	Z=26
I=9	R=18	

The Jewish gematria is somewhat more complicated, but according to the table below you will quickly understand its logic. There multiple Hebrew gematria methods but it looks like only the standard one is used in mass media.

THE HEBREW ALPHABET

consists of 22 (2 × 11) letters, so the 5 finals were added to make up three series of 9, or 27 in all:

Aleph	א	= 1	Yod	י	= 10	Koph	ק	= 100	
Beth	ב	= 2	Kaph	כ	= 20	Resh	ר	= 200	
Gimel	ג	= 3	Lamed	ל	= 30	Shin	ש	= 300	
Daleth	ד	= 4	Mem	מ	= 40	Tau	ת	= 400	
He	ה	= 5	Nun	נ	= 50	Koph	ך	= 500	
Vau	ו	= 6	Samech	ס	= 60	Mem	ם	= 600	Finals.
Zayin	ז	= 7	Ayin	ע	= 70	Nun	ן	= 700	
Cheth	ח	= 8	Pe	פ	= 80	Pe	ף	= 800	
Teth	ט	= 9	Tsaddi	צ	= 90	Tsaddi	ץ	= 900	

The updated Pythagorean conversion table uses numbers 1 through 9, each of which is related to certain letters of the alphabet. An alternate version is the updated Chaldean Conversion Table which works in a similar way except it is numbered 1 to 8 and the letters associated with each number are different as well.

Pythagorean English Gematria Chart:

A=1	J=1	S=1/10
B=2	K=2/11	T=2
C=3	L=3	U=3
D=4	M=4	V=4/22
E=5	N=5	W=5
F=6	O=6	X=6
G=7	P=7	Y=7
H=8	Q=8	Z=8
I=9	R=9	

Chaldean Numerology

1	2	3	4	5	6	7	8
A	B	C	D	E	U	O	F
I	K	G	M	H	V	Z	P
J	R	L	T	N	W		
Q		S		X			
Y							

In Greek, each unit (1, 2, …, 9) was assigned a separate letter, each tens (10, 20, …, 90) a separate letter, and each hundreds (100, 200, …, 900) a separate letter. This requires 27 letters, so the 24-letter alphabet was extended by using three obsolete letters: digamma ⬚,(also used are stigma ⬚ or, in modern Greek, στ) for 6, qoppa ⬚ for 90, and sampi ⬚ for 900.

This alphabetic system operates on the additive principle in which the numeric values of the letters are added together to form the total. For example, 241 is represented as σμα (200 + 40 + 1).

A	α	1.	I	ι	10.	P	ρ	100.
B	β	2.	K	κ	20.	Σ	σ	200.
Γ	γ	3.	Λ	λ	30.	T	τ	300.
Δ	δ	4.	M	μ	40.	Y	υ	400.
E	ε	5.	N	ν	50.	Φ	φ	500.
	ς	6.	Ξ	ξ	60.	X	χ	600.
Z	ζ	7.	O	ο	70.	Ψ	ψ	700.
H	η	8.	Π	π	80.	Ω	ω	800.
Θ	ϑ	9.	ϟ	ϛ	90.		⟩	900.

In Sumerian (also called English) each following letter is assigned value by adding 6 to the previous one starting from 6 to 156.

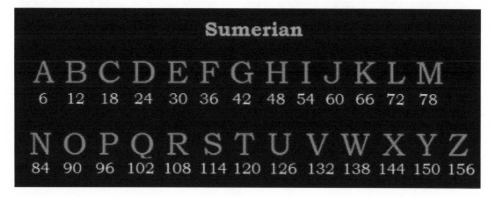

In modern ciphers related to pop culture and the media, all these Gematric systems used combined, when in the same text one encounters encoded words by several systems. I believe that if only one of the coding methods was constantly used, then even unprepared people could easily take notice of it. Employment of the different systems gives to their authors plausible deniability. Probably, the inverse method may also be used, when the numbers can be considered as letters (gematria calculator will give you hundreds of words with the same numerical value), but I did not even consider such a method, since this would be similar to pure guess work resembling a cherry picking. There quite a few researchers who are trying to fit the right words (in their opinion) in to the context using the choice offered by the gematria calculator.

Chapter VI Donald Trump and "Back to the Future"

So, lets us try to employ gematria to Donald Trump and other real and fictitious characters. In order to do this, you do not have to sit and add up numbers manually. There are quite a few on and offline gematria calculators in existence. By simply entering text there you will be able to calculate a digital value in various numerological systems in a matter of seconds.

Trump-in simple gematria has a numerical value of 88. With a middle initial J(John) -888. Interesting "coincidences"?

120 108 126 78 96

Trump in Simple Gematria Equals: **88** (t r u m p)
20 18 21 13 16

יהוה Results by Jewish Gematria

This is how he uses his Twitter account with middle initial J

Donald J. Trump ✓
@realDonaldTrump

45th President of the United States of America ▮▮

⊙ Washington, DC

⧉ Instagram.com/realDonaldTrump

▦ Joined March 2009

Donald J Trump

$$\left(\frac{d \quad o \quad n \quad al \quad d \quad j \quad t \quad r \quad u \quad m \quad p}{24 \; 90 \; 84 \; 6 \; 72 \; 24 \; ^0 \; 60 \; ^0 \; 120 \; 108 \; 126 \; 78 \; 96} \right)$$

in English Gematria Equals: **888**

Exactly on September 11, 2002 (911) and not a day later, Donald Trump acquires the Bedminster golf course with a mansion, which used to belong to no one other than John Delorean, the maker of the "time machine" from " Back to the Future " DMC 12. The purchase was reported by the media on the next day. DeLorean and his former wife, model/actress Cristina Ferrare, bought the property in 1981, just as the former General Motors wunderkind was launching the manufacture of his distinctive stainless steel sports car with gull-wing doors. As history now knows, the DeLorean Motor Company failed, and DeLorean was charged with cocaine trafficking in an attempt to raise money for his car company.

Although DeLorean was eventually acquitted, the ordeal cost him his marriage and his financial stability. For years before the bankruptcy, he battled with creditors to avoid foreclosure on the estate. It is known that Trump paid $ 35 million for the property and two years later the club was open to visitors. So, this is other clear and undeniable link between Donald Trump and the plot of BTF.

← → C ⌂ ⓘ www.newjerseyhills.com/trump-buying-bedminster-golf-course/article_1a108d11-e74a-56dd-9f9f-4b334ad03b2b.html

🏠 Our Newspapers   Advertise   Classifieds   About Us   Entertainment   Photo Gallery   Subscribe   Sub

‹ PREV

Trump buying Bedminster golf course

Sep 12, 2002 💬 0

f 🐦 ✉ 🖨 🔖

BEDMINSTER TWP. - New York real estate mogul Donald Trump is buying the former John Z. DeLorean estate off Lamington Road, site of a foundering golf course construction project.

Trump confirmed Tuesday afternoon that he is the buyer of the 506-acre estate known as Lamington Farm, which was approved by the township in August 2001 for use as a golf course and country club.

"Yes, I've bought it as of today," said Trump, who owns golf courses in Florida and Westchester County, N.Y. "It's a wonderful piece of property and it will be absolutely a world class golf course."

John DeLorean and his DMC 12

Eric Trump and his wife Lara in Bedminster

After discovering such strange "coincidences" of Trump's connection to the number 88, I had to study purposefully the entire history of the appearance of the number 88 next to the name of Trumps for many years. That's what came out of it:

In December 2016, the media reported the death of the 88-year-old tailor of Donald Trump, Martin Greenfield, who, according to the note, was tailoring also for several previous US presidents.

THE 88-YEAR-OLD TAILOR WHO DRESSES TRUMP AND OBAMA IS SUING BROOKS BROTHERS

In Daily Commute by MR Magazine Staff / December 7, 2016 / Leave a Comment

The 88-year-old tailor whose handmade suits have been worn by everyone from President Eisenhower to President-elect Trump delivered a different kind of suit to Brooks Brothers this week. Martin Greenfield, founder of Martin Greenfield Clothiers, sued the luxury menswear chain on Monday, alleging his company lost nearly $2 million in revenue and income due to a breach of contract. Greenfield claims that that he and Brooks Brothers had a verbal agreement that stipulated Brooks Brothers would give him one year's notice before ending their business relationship. Greenfield had been making Brooks Brothers' Golden Fleece line of suits for more than two decades, according to the suit. Read more at *Fortune*.

Personal aircraft of Donald Trump Boeing 757 turned out to have 88 windows in contrast to the standard model.

In September 2016, Trump received endorsement from 88 senior military commanders of the US Army:

Son of Donald, Eric Trump managed to spend on his logging at the hotel $ 88,000, during a visit to Uruguay, where he was promoting the project of Tramp Tower

ⓘ www.nydailynews.com/news/politics/state-department-spent-15-000-trump-hotel-article-1.3321117

≡   SHARE THIS f 🐦 ✉

The Post previously reported on the Secret Service spending more than $88,000 on lodging when Eric Trump visited Uruguay in January to promote a Trump Tower that is under construction.

Prestigious magazine Economist reported with reference to RBC (respectable Russian business journal) that: "RBC reports that the mention of Trump in the analytical programs of the Russian federal television fell by 88%." I was personally unable to find a single line on this account in the Russian-language news reports of RBC. Story appeared to be concocted in order to link one more time Trumps name and number 88.

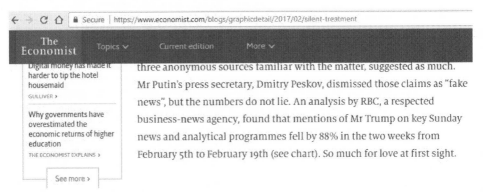

← → C ⟲   🔒 Secure | https://www.economist.com/blogs/graphicdetail/2017/02/silent-treatment

The Economist   Topics ⌄   Current edition   More ⌄

Digital money has made it harder to tip the hotel housemaid
GULLIVER ›

Why governments have overestimated the economic returns of higher education
THE ECONOMIST EXPLAINS ›

See more ›

three anonymous sources familiar with the matter, suggested as much. Mr Putin's press secretary, Dmitry Peskov, dismissed those claims as "fake news", but the numbers do not lie. An analysis by RBC, a respected business-news agency, found that mentions of Mr Trump on key Sunday news and analytical programmes fell by 88% in the two weeks from February 5th to February 19th (see chart). So much for love at first sight.

"Trump is most googled person in 88 countries" Time Magazine

See the Most Googled Person in Each Country in 2016

By DAVID JOHNSON and MEGAN MCCLUSKEY December 22, 2016

People across the globe were more curious about Donald Trump than anyone else this year. The president-elect earned the distinction of being the top-trending person in 88 countries in 2016, far more places than anyone else in the world, according to data Google provided to TIME.

The right Internet portal Breitbart says that "according to the results of a public opinion poll, 88% of Trump voters agree that the media is an enemy of the Americans."

"88% of the media are hostile to Trump during his first month in the White House"

👍 Like 14.3M   Friday, Mar 2

𝕸𝖆𝖎𝖑 Online

Home | **News** | U.S. | Sport | TV&Showbiz | Australia | Femail | Health | Science | Money | Vi
Latest Headlines | News | World News | Arts | Headlines | France | Pictures | Most read | Wires | Discounts

'No honeymoon for the president': Three major networks' coverage of Trump in his first month in office was '88 percent hostile'

- Right-leaning Media Research Center conducted study on Trump coverage
- It said ABC, NBC, and CBS newscasts were '88 percent hostile' to new president
- First month of Trump administration marred by controversial executive orders

By ARIEL ZILBER FOR DAILYMAIL.COM
PUBLISHED: 22:25 GMT, 2 March 2017 | UPDATED: 22:48 GMT, 2 March 2017

A list of similar coincidences can be continued to the infinity. It is much more important to investigate the circumstances that will indicate that Donald Trump is personally aware of his connection with the code 88 and has a direct relationship to it. Such fact, were available almost immediately since I already knew what to look for:

The gematria calculator reveals that the design of electoral slogans, both of Trump himself and his rival Hillary Clinton has been also calculated according to code 88, and therefore designated for Trump personally as a bearer of gematria 88. The slogans of both candidates had numerical value of 88. Neither the name Hillary nor her surname or both combined, do not have such a numerical value. All that shows that the outcome of the election was predetermined long before t, and most likely, both candidates, despite their acting skills in public were aware of that.

"Make America Great Again 2016"

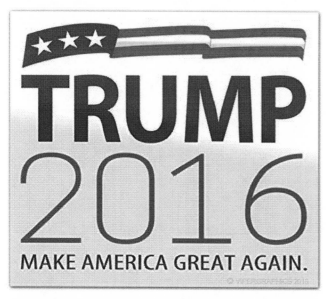

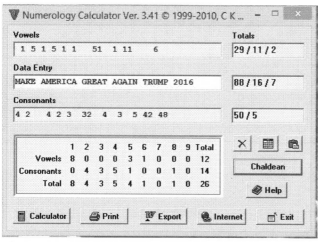

The electoral slogan of Hillary Clinton "Stronger Together" -88. Moreover, the logo of her campaign represents H and 11 thus 8x11=88

I don't think it is too far-fetched to state that this logo is reminiscent of twin towers with arrow representing plane intersecting them. Perhaps it wasn't intended by the creators, but it certainly fits the bill.

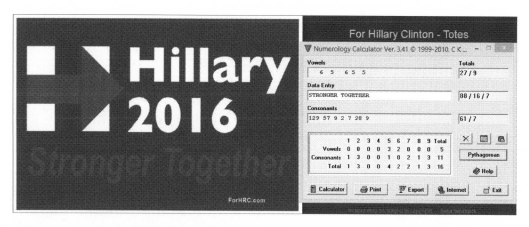

Hillary Clinton released the book "Hard Choices," in 2015 in which she described her 88 most difficult life dilemmas.

nymag.com/daily/intelligencer/2014/06/88-choices-in-hillary-clintons-hard-choices.html

Intelligencer / EARLY AND AWKWARD

88 Choices in Hillary Clinton's *Hard Choices*

By Joe Coscarelli

June 10, 2014
3:51 pm

f Share

Tweet

Comment

Photo: Simon & Schuster

Journalists estimated that during a meeting with employees of the company Whitney Brothers in the state of New Hampshire Hillary Clinton uttered "hm"88 times. The clip was compiled with an exact calculation of the sacramental interjection. I do not know if Hillary framed herself that way, or she was framed by "script writers", but it all happened on April 20, that is, on the birthday of Adolf Hitler. Heil Hitler (HH = 88). I don't see the other reason why to break such a ridiculous news otherwise.

  0:49 / 0:59

88 Times Hillary Clinton Said 'Mmm Hmm' in New Hampshire | SUPERcuts! #188

174,308 views   👍 417   👎 37   ↪ SHARE   ⊟₊   ...

 Washington Free Beacon

To top it all, the elections were scheduled for 8.11.2016, date with numerology 88 11x88 = 88 Trump's victory was announced the very next day, on the date with numerology 911, that is 9.11.2016. So, did Trump know about his connection with the number 88? Look at the phone number of SMS for Trump support during his campaign-88022, that is, 88 and 22, the number which is result of division of 88(88/4), which is also allowed according to numerological rules.

Google indicates the height of Donald Trump as 1 meter and 88 centimeters. Naturally, all of the above should not necessarily reflect the reality, but the media continues to steer the numbers in the direction they need (more precisely, those who control them). Now Google indicate different height 190 centimeters. Not so long ago there were contradicting reports about the Trump's weight and these numbers also reeked of the heavy manipulation, I suspect not only for the sake of reducing the weight in attempts to hide the obesity.

Trump Plaza in Jersey City located on 88 Morgan street

See photos   See outside

Trump Plaza ★

Website   Directions

3.7 ★★★★★ 30 Google reviews

Apartment building in Jersey City, New Jersey

Trump Plaza also known as Trump Plaza Residences, is the first of two planned apartment complex buildings to be built in Jersey City, New Jersey. Trump Plaza Residences is 532 ft tall and has 55 floors. Wikipedia

Address: 88 Morgan St, Jersey City, NJ 07302, USA

Floors: 55

Height: 162 m

Construction started: 2006

Opened: 2008

Floor area: 16 ha

In the popular in the 90s series "Suddenly Susan" with Brooke Shields in the title role, most of the action took place in the editorial office of a fictional magazine. t Donald Trump made a cameo appearance. In one of the episodes the heroes decided to make a sensational magazine cover featuring a photo of Donald Trump with an inscription: "Our next president?" By pure chance, of course, the gematria of this visionary phrase showed 88.

our next president = 3+6+9+4+4+3+7+2+9+4+8+9+5+4+4+7 = 88
(Reverse Reduced)

In May 2016 the world's media circulated a fake obituary of 88-year-old Trump's cousin with a posthumous appeal "not to vote for a scoundrel." I think that the true goal of the demarche was another proclamation of the number 88 next to Trump's name, and not so much the denigration of the presidential candidate by such a clumsy fake.

In November 1987, Donald Trump releases the book under the title The Art of the Deal with Gematria 888.

Gematria 88 also explains that to play Donald Trump in the movie was chosen no other than Johnny Depp"

''Over the course of his eclectic and wide-ranging career, Johnny Depp has played some evil characters, from his recent role as gangster Whitey Bulger in *Black Mass* to his portrayal of the bloodthirsty Victorian-era hairstylist Sweeney Todd. But his newest character—a racist, megalomaniacal, misogynistic real estate developer—may be his darkest. In a new, 50-minute video produced by Funny or Die, Depp plays Donald Trump. The "lost film" is a satirical adaptation of Trump's 1987 *New York Times* bestseller *The Art of the Deal*.
The movie presents itself as a never-seen, long-lost movie of the week starring and directed by Trump that was pre-empted by a *Monday Night Football* game. *Donald Trump's The Art of the Deal: The Movie* was directed by Oscar nominee Adam McKay (*The Big Short*) and stars Depp, Alfred Molina, Michaela Watkins, ALF, Patton Oswalt, and Stephen Merchant, among others. "The plan was to move really fast because we thought Trump would go away, at least as a presidential

candidate," Funny or Die editor in chief Owen Burke told The New York Times. "When he bizarrely didn't go away, we had a little more time. But that meant keeping the secret for longer."
New York Times February 2016"

The Art of the Deal = 120+48+30 + 6+108+120 + 90+36 + 120+48+30 + 24+30+6+72 = **888** (Sumerian)

Donald J. Trump = 24+90+84+6+72+24 + 60 + 120+108+126+78+96 = **888** (Sumerian)

John Depp in Simple Gematria Equals: **88** ($\frac{j}{10}\ \frac{o}{15}\ \frac{hn}{8\ 14}\ ^0\ \frac{dep\ p}{4\ 5\ 16\ 16}$)

In his 2004 book "The Way Up" Donald Trump reveals us that he studied Kabbala for a long time with the famous teacher Eitan Yardeni from Israel, who taught Kabbala to Madonna and other celebrities. It is noteworthy that Trump made this revelation on page 188 of the book.

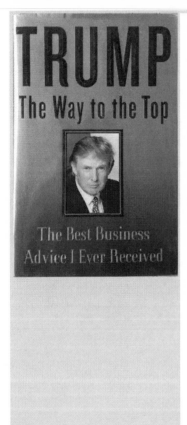

TRUMP
The Way to the Top

The Best Business
Advice I Ever Received

Guy OSEARY

Copartner and CEO of Maverick Recording Company

Four people have given me sound nuggets of wisdom that have helped me keep business in perspective.

When I was nineteen, I complained to David Geffen about some other people in the entertainment business who were making a lot of money and who I didn't think deserved it. David turned to me and said, "You need to be a racehorse. Do you know what racehorses do?" I answered, "They race." David replied, "No, they wear blinders! If they looked to the left or right, they would lose. Don't look to the left and don't look to the right. Wear blinders and race your own race!"

Never lose perspective

One day, when my Kabbalah teacher, Eitan Yardeni, asked how I was doing, I told him I needed a break. I was thoroughly exhausted, overwhelmed, and overworked. Eitan then said, "Do you know what you should do now?" I thought he was going to encourage me to take some time off. But instead he replied, "No, go work harder! Be careful what you ask for because you may get it." Eitan was right. If I ask for a break, God may hear me and I may get one—a long one. I took this advice to heart and started to work even harder.

188

The ex-wife of Donald Trump Marla Maples does not hide that she has been studying Kabbalah for more than 20 years. On the photo below, she is depicted with a paper bag bearing the emblem of the Kabbalistic center.

Got*C*eleb

''Madonna is on her way to the Holy Land. The pop diva, a student of Jewish mysticism, is headed to Israel on a spiritual quest for the Jewish New Year, which begins at sundown today (Sept. 15).

Madonna is on her way to the Holy Land. The pop diva, a student of Jewish mysticism, is headed to Israel on a spiritual quest for the Jewish New Year, which begins at sundown today (Sept. 15).

Her five-day visit, which includes trips to graves of rabbinical sages, brought a diversion to a country normally focused on the conflict with the Palestinians. Israelis reacted with a mix of excitement, bewilderment and anger.

Madonna isn't Jewish but has taken an interest in Kabbalah, or Jewish mysticism, in recent years. She has adopted the Hebrew name Esther, wears a red thread on her wrist to ward off the evil eye and reportedly refuses to perform on the Jewish Sabbath.

She also has incorporated Jewish symbols into some of her music videos, much to the consternation of many religious leaders. The organization hosting her in Israel has ordered news reporters to wear white clothes and not to take notes when covering her appearances during the New Year's holiday, or Rosh Hashanah.

"This is entertainment, not Judaism," quipped Uri Orbach, a popular talk-radio host.

Madonna is joining a group of 2,000 other students of Jewish mysticism from 22 countries, according to the Kabbalah Center, the sponsor of the trip. **Designer Donna Karan and Donald Trump's ex-wife Marla Maples are among the other celebrities expected to attend.** Reports Billboard in September 2004"

In the light of all of the above it did not surprise me when I discovered that gematria of Marla Maples is 666. Probably, among of others it was one of the criteria for Donald Trump to marry her.

The media reported that on Day 88 (what a remarkable date, is it not?) of his presidency, Trump appeared on the balcony of the White House, accompanied by an Easter bunny, during the traditional Easter eggs roll on the South lawn. We'll talk about the Easter bunny later.

113

Day 88/April 17th - President Donald Trump, joined by the
Easter Bunny, speaks from the Truman Balcony during the
annual White House Easter Egg Roll on the South Lawn of
the White House in Washington.

CREDIT: AP PHOTO/CAROLYN KAST

By the way, in another of the obvious parodies of Donald
Trump in the film "Lego" 2014-President Business from
Octan Corporation (**octo i**n Greek-**8**), which tried to
enslave the whole world, even by appearance
unmistakably resembled Trump. Headquarters of the
President Business served the Octane Tower (an obvious
hint at the Trump Tower)

Let's go back to the film "Back to the Future" for a while. In addition to "88 miles per hour" and the prototype of Donald Trump, there were other indicators of the code 88, which, unlike those, were not intended to draw attention. Note the position of the hands of the clock in the beginning of movie. From the very first minutes, the clocks appear on the screen, where the hands are clearly showing 8 and 11 (8x11 = 88)

It is noteworthy that the same actors who play in movies where a certain code is involved continue to appear in other films, with the same codes, decades later. The directors of these films may be completely different. For example, Emmet Brown, "Dock" from "Back to the Future", actor Christopher Lloyd, starred in the thriller "88" in 2015, that is exactly 30 years after his first-time travel in BTF in 2015, but with completely different director.

Pay attention that even here both clock's hands are on the 8

According to the movie plot in BTF, a lightning bolt stopped the clock on the city tower on 10:04 November 14, 1955 (30 years before the main action of the film in1985). Why this is not a random time you will find out below.

SAVE THE CLOCK TOWER

The Weather
Today — A slight atmospheric disturbance of unidentified origin is reported over Hova Scotia, causing a low pressure area to move down rather rapidly over the northwestern states, bringing a forecast of rain, accompanied by winds of light gale force. Maximum temperature 66, minimum 44.

Hill Valley Telegraph

Index
Business ... 52 | Local ... 47
Classified ... 47 | Movies ... 43
Comics ... 41 | Radio ... 43
Crossword ... 54 | Sports ... 48
Editorial ... 49 | World ... 54

Vol. XVII, No. 32   COMPLETE NEWS SERVICE R. T. F. NEWS WIRE   MONDAY, NOVEMBER 14, 1955   THE NEWSPAPER THE PEOPLE DEPEND UPON   10¢

CLOCK TOWER STRUCK BY LIGHTNING

CLOCK STOPPED AT 10:04

Hill Valley's landmark Clock Tower was struck by lightning during the weekend's freak electrical storm. The lightning bolt fused the clock's internal mechanism and stopped the clock's hands, perhaps permanently, at 10:04 PM.

The strike occurred during the peak of the unexpected lightning storm. Experts and city officials have been surveying the damage since yesterday morning, and it was not yet clear if it could be repaired.

"It's difficult to say at this point," said Brad Curtier, the clock's chief custodian. "The lightning bolt fused a lot of the old clockwork, and we're investigating the possibility of repair. Personally, I can tell you that it doesn't look good. I'd be surprised if we ever got it working again."

The peculiar failure of the building's lightning rod is under investigation. Under normal circumstances, it provides sufficient electrical grounding to safely and harmlessly absorb lightning strikes. Investigators found the rod had somehow become completely severed from the grounding circuit. Theories as to how this happened have

not been forthcoming.

"It's the darnedest thing," said electrician Murray Graham of Gus & Andrew's Electrical Repair, Inc. while assessing the damage. "I've seen plenty of lightning strikes in my day, and I know that if this bit wasn't grounded at all you should have had damage to a lot more than just the clockwork. Where the heck did all that extra power from the bolt go?"

Graham isn't the only expert mystified by the circumstances. Local scientist Dr. Emmett Brown had been conducting a delicate experiment during the strike, and narrowly escaped injury as his invention met an untimely end.

"I was performing a trial of some new, specialized weather-sensing equipment of my own design, and the lightning struck at the precise moment to, well, destroy it," said Dr. Brown as he collected the scorched remains of some cables from the area last night. "I did damage to gather some, shall I say, extremely promising data regarding my work, but sadly it will be a long time before I'm able to undertake that particular experiment again."

The clock's future may be uncertain, but its past is well-documented. It was ceremonially started during a town festival at 8:00 PM, September 5, 1885, and installed in the courthouse when the building was completed. The Mayor dedicated the clock to the people of Hill County with a proclamation; "May it stand for all time."

Plans To Launch Tests of New Toll System Here

Commuters will find themselves greeted by new tolls on local bridges and tunnels, if a measure under consideration by legislators comes to pass.

"This plan will subsidize the upkeep of the facilities," said Mayor Thomas. "As Hill Valley grows and the new housing developments get underway, avenues such as the River Road tunnel and the bridges over the local ravines will become major thoroughfares."

The progressive motion was criticized by Hill Valley board members Bob Vincent, Dot Net.
Continued on Page 26

For over 70 years, the Hill Valley Courthouse Clock has served as a constant timekeeper and landmark for Hill Valley residents and visitors. The clock now only displays 10:04, the time Saturday night when it was rendered inoperable by a bolt of lightning during a freak electrical storm. *Photo: Gale Zemeckis*

PLEASE MAKE DONATIONS TO
The Hill Valley Preservation Society

In the time machine, 88 are simultaneously displayed on the dashboard with 10:04 on the alarm clock.

10.04 can be interpreted as on October 4 (Americans display the month before the date). As I've mentioned above in numerology the order of the digits or their fractionality can be disregarded. October 4 = 104 - 277th day of the year (278th in leap years) in the Gregorian calendar. 88 days left to the end of the year. It is possible that 104 is a completely separate code, but it always appears beside 88, and as you can see, it is directly connected to it. I've analyzed hundreds of films and everywhere code 88 went hand in hand with code 104.

On the old photo Doc Brown is depicted in 1885 with the clock tower on the background, where the hand showing 8 hours and 8 minutes. Very skillfully was chosen the name of the Christopher Lloyd's hero - Dr. Emmett Lathrop Brown-read the name backwards and you will get "Time Portal" (you just need to phonetically simplify the name to Emit). Similar semantic tricks are often found in coded texts.

88 and 10:04 shown together on the dashboard of the time machine Delorean DMC 12

In another film starring Michael J. Fox from BTF, which was released on 1.04 1988 (which is also noteworthy, 104 and 88) the close up of the clock displays 10.04, as well as the twin towers on the background of which the main character reflects on **"new world"**.

In the film " The Adventures of Buckaroo Banzai across the **8th** Dimension ", Christopher Lloyd the very same " Doc " Brown from the BTF, continues the theme of 88. It seems that he was casted in these roles because of his date of birth that. He was born on October 22, 2010. 2 + 2 = 4 and 10 with necessary 104 in numerology to be casted in 88- 104 movies.

88 displayed on the license plate and the door of the truck

The engine fires with the switch in position of the clock hands 10 and 4.

The greatest concentration of codes 88 and 104 is in films about time travel and portals to other dimensions. The code 911 or images of twin towers are also indispensable satellites of these codes.

For example, a film with the absurd title of "Being John Malkovich", where the characters discover a portal to another world in the gap between the floors and it happened to be an 8th floor. Gematria of the very title of the film equals 88. If you think that method of using gematria for decoding codes is completely ridiculous, and you consider its results totally coincidental, then simply take any name or the title of the film, then try to run them through gematria calculator. After that you will see for yourself how insignificant are the chances of any random coincidences if you are looking for them in the places where the were not intended to be.

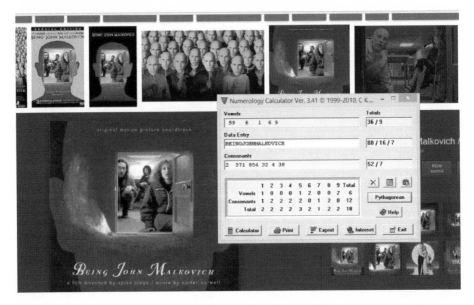

The psychiatrist shows to the John Cusack's hero 2 stylized "8". Later I will explain what they are.

The clock hands are at 10 and 4

Unbelievable but the true, on the current and previous
hundred dollar bills, the clock towers hands indicating the
same figures. I sifted through a lot of literature on the
history of design of banknotes, but nowhere to be found
an explanation on why these particular hand positions
were chosen. One hand is at 10 (X), the other at 6 (VI = IV),

that is 4. In this case, the Roman numerals VI IV are a mirror image of each other and are therefore interchangeable.

On the excerpt below my statement about hands position is confirmed and also absence of information why this particular time was chosen. Beside curious number 11.9%(911) is present linking 104/88 to 911.

SMART SHOPPING   QUIZZES   LISTS   VIDEOS   AMAZING FACTS   ⬚ SHOI

6. The $100 bill represents 11.9 percent of all U.S. paper currency production, with the average bill expected to last 89 months in circulation."''"

7. The clock on the back of a $100 bill shows the time as 4:10. According to the Bureau of Engraving and Printing, "There are no records explaining why that particular time was chosen."

The new Freedom Tower (One World Trade Center), which now stands on the site of the twin towers has **104** floors. Even its the postal code as well as her predecessor-twin towers is 10048. Nike in their 2011 commercial, featuring the theme of the movie "Back to the Future", The Lone pine mall (Freedom Tower) on the digital clock next to the time 10:04.

In another film about traveling through time and space- " Event Horizon " the hero of Lawrence Fishburne pulls the object from the box with the code LXXXVIII = 88 Roman numerals.

In the popular TV series "Spin City" both the actors from "Back to the Future" appear together in an episode titled "Back to the Future." Judgment Day". In addition to many astrotheological remarks (on which we will not focus now), the episode features insider jokes from the BTF and the rating of the series on the website of the International Movie Database(IMDB) is coincidentally 8.8. By chance of course, particularly there Donald Trump makes his cameo appearance.

Another film about time travel "Hot tub time machine"
also contains codes 88 and 104. Besides on remote control
panel appears 666. In this movie 88 and 104 are also
indirectly linked to code word "nuclear" which also
present in different forms (key word nuclear or different
concepts involving other similar words such a atomic). In
this case is the whole event occurred thanks to the Russian
energy drink called Chernobyl-place of the worst nuclear
disaster in 1986.

"Three separated, down-on-their-luck friends: Adam Yates
is dumped by his girlfriend; Nick Webber-Agnew is a
henpecked husband with a dead-end job; and Lou Dorchen
is a party animal in his 40s. They reconnect when Lou is
hospitalized for carbon monoxide poisoning. To cheer him
up, Adam and Nick arrange for Lou to join them at Kodiak
Valley Ski Resort, where the three enjoyed good times in

their youth; Adam's shut-in nephew Jacob tags along. During a night of heavy drinking in their hotel room's hot tub, the four douse the console with an illegal Russian energy drink called Chernobyl. The next day, the friends go skiing and, after many strange occurrences (1980s fashion, music videos on MTV and Michael Jackson still being black), they realize they have traveled back to 1986. Adam, Lou and Nick have also assumed their younger bodies: they appear normal to each other, but to others (and in their reflections) they look like their younger selves. Jacob's appearance has not changed, though he occasionally flickers."

Heroes wear the mask of President Reagan (gematria 104) and Queen Elizabeth (88)

RONALD REAGAN = 17+14+13+1+11+4 + 17+5+1+7+1+13 = **104** (Jewish Ordinal)

ELIZABETH = 5+12+9+26+1+2+5+20+8 = **88**

In the thriller '88 minutes' with Al Pacino the date of birth of the main character is September 11 (911), 1960. Next shown a fragment of a television interview with the villain shortly before his execution. In the corner of the screen you see the time- 11:06 (911). Remember the rules of numerology, where the order of the digits is not important and 6 = 9.

Watch hands on 11 and 6 (911)

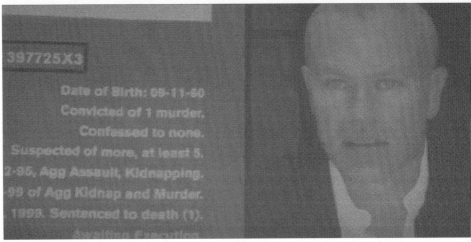

Another character in the movie was born on 911 date-June 11 ,1959, expiry date of the driver's license shows similar date.

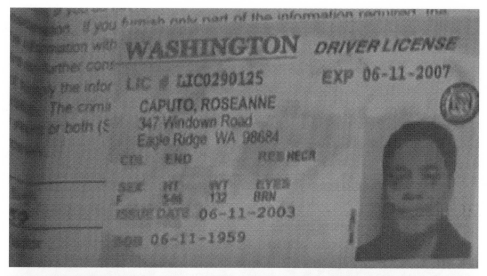

According to the movie plot Al Pacino's hero must die at
11.45 = 119 (911)

88 Minutes Script - transcript from the screenplay and/or Al Pacino Movie
www.script-o-rama.com/movie_scripts/e/88-minutes-script-transcript-pacino.html ▾
You have **88 minutes** to live. What? You know how long **88 minutes** can be, don't you? That's **11:45**
AM. Who is this? Tick tock. - Who the hell is this? - Tick tock. What are you sayin'? Hey Michael, wait
up. Jack Gramm Associates. I want you to set a trap and a trace on my cell. What's going on? Contact
our wireless carrier.

Close up on 911 on the fire truck

Homer Helmcken-HH-88, real billboard in Vancouver
purposely filmed on the background of Porsche 911

Chapter XVII. Donnie Darko-Donald Trump

However, the most interesting and conceptual film after "Back to the Future", which combined not only the codes 88 and 911, but also allusions to the upcoming presidency of Donald Trump is "Donnie Darko." Released on **19.01**.01 (911) with Jake Gyllenhaal in the title role, film quickly acquired a cult status.

The action takes place in October of **1988** in a small American town, shortly before the **presidential election**. High school student Donnie Darko lives with his parents, older and younger sisters. October 2, he wakes up and leaves the house on the mental order of a man in the suit of a huge rabbit with an ominous grin, introduced himself by the name "Frank". Frank warns that in 28 days, 6 hours, 42 minutes and 12 seconds (28 + 6 + 42 + 12 = 88) "the world will end". Donnie Darko is an **eighth-grader** who had a dog that died when he was **8** years old.

In the morning, Donnie wakes up on the golf course and upon returning home, discovers that at night a huge engine of the plane fell on his house, hitting directly into Donny's room. His older sister, Elizabeth, tells that the investigators of the Federal Aviation Administration do not know where the engine came from.

The artistic world of the film is built on the principles of magical realism, similar to such series as "Twin Peaks." Unlike many similar films, surreal events can be explained. For this purpose, throughout the film are scattered quotes from the treatise of Roberta on travel in time. On the official DVD the director thoroughly explains the details of the construction of this world. Donny's dialogues with his teacher discusses issues of time travel, **mentions are made of the famous Delorean DMS-12 and the film "Back to the Future".**

In addition to the obvious "coincidence" of Donnie-Donald names, Darko wears a T-shirt with a **Triumph** motorcycle. If you look in the Oxford English Dictionary, you will find out that the word "tramp" in the 16th century meant **"triumph."**

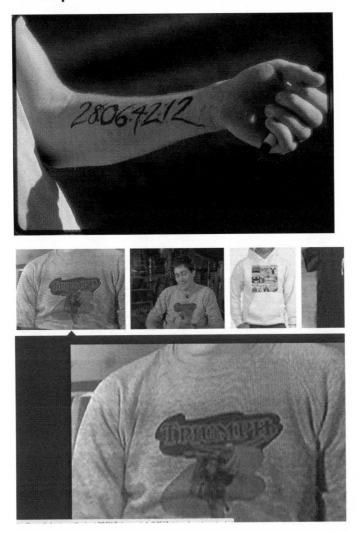

Trump meaning in the Oxford English language dictionary

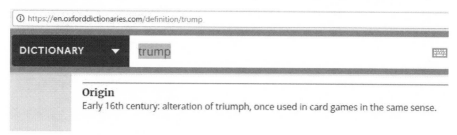

Attention of the viewer is accentuated on the fact that the 1988 presidential elections are taking place. On the screen flashes a bottle of Donald Darko's medication with the word "Win" and 1988 and Donald underneath. An obvious allusion on the winner of the elections and bearer of the 88 number which is Donald Trump. Seems improbable but this is how game is played and you will see other allusions.

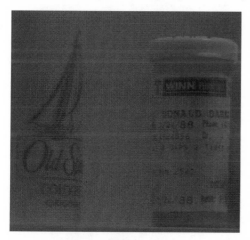

TV report on the elections of 1988 which were won by George H.W. Bush on 8.11.88

Even the full date on a vial sums up to 24 + 7 + 88 = 119 which is exactly gematria of name Donald

Donald = 4+50+40+1+20+4 = **119** (Jewish)

(6 letters, 1 word)

A scene in the cinema where the prophetic hallucinations of Donnie Darko begin when the clock is shown on the cinema screen with hands on 10 and

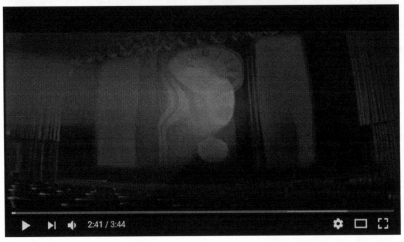

Donnie Darko - Theater Scene

Donnie shown on the background of the movie poster "The Last Temptation of **Christ**" by Martin Scorsese. The film was released in the **8.08.88**

The Greek gematria or isopsephy of the word Jesus is exactly 888

$$I = 10$$
$$H = 8$$
$$\Sigma = 200$$
$$O = 70$$
$$Y = 400$$
$$\underline{\Sigma = 200}$$
$$888$$

During entire movie in front of Donnie's house is parked Porsche 911 and does not take any part in the plot, except of the intended manifestation of the code 911

Later, Jake Gyllenhaal will appear in the film "Source Code," where the hero also makes a journey through time. A soldier wakes up in someone else's body and discovers he's part of an experimental government program to find the bomber of a commuter train. A mission he has only **8** minutes to complete. The film was released on **1.04**. 11, that is code 104.

Why this actor was casted in the movies with time travel themes and codes 88-104? Perhaps the answer is in the gematria 88 of his full name-Jacob Benjamin Gyllenhaal

Jacob Benjamin Gyllenhaal =
1+1+3+6+2+2+5+5+1+1+4+9+5+7+7+3+3+5+5+8+1+1+3 = 88 (Reduced)

Both watch hands on 8=88

The is a strong connection between Trump and twin towers. Donald Trump was active in the discussion of the events of September 11, 2001 from the very first days. Then and afterwards he made several controversial statements. Trump believes that the twin towers were able to withstand the direct hit of the aircraft. On September 13, 2001, he gave an interview to the NBC News channel, which hinted at the possible use of explosives for the controlled demolition of the World Trade Center: "I happen to think they had not only a plane but bombs that exploded almost simultaneously, because I can't imagine anything being able to go through that wall. Most buildings are built where the steel is on the inside around the elevator shaft. This one was built from the outside, which is the strongest structure you can have, and it [came down] almost just like a can of soup."

Early 80s interview of Donald Trump while overflying in the helicopter Manhattan with the view of twin towers. While flying he mentioned his plans to purchase the twin towers. By the way, famous Manhattan Project for the creation of first atomic bomb in the 1940s prominently features twin towers on its logo.

A few years ago, he even appeared in quite silly commercial for the chain of his hotels with sheep numbered 9 and 11 next to each other.

Even in some films long before the events of 11.9.01, where Trump's parody characters were present, he was always accompanied by the code 911. For example, the tycoon developer Daniel Clamp from Gremlins. The scene in his office was filmed in the twin towers of the WTC, and from the outside the office was a copy of the Trump Tower.

Right tycoon developer Daniel Clump (Trump), interviewed by correspondents with microphones on which 9 and 11 (911) are visible. On the right, one of the reporters holding microphone is Eric Shawn, a real correspondent for Fox News, who 11 years later will report on the burning twin towers (insert in the upper left corner).

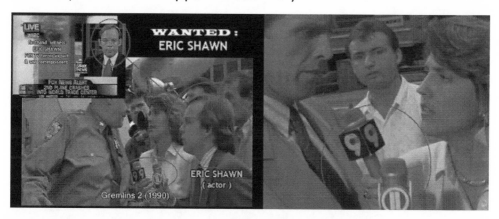

Eric Shawn in the later years on channel Fox News

For completeness of the picture with the microphones of the channels 9 and 11, in the movie "Gremlins 2" there are also real twins present. That was done in order to associate in the audience's subcortex the number 911 and **twin** towers.

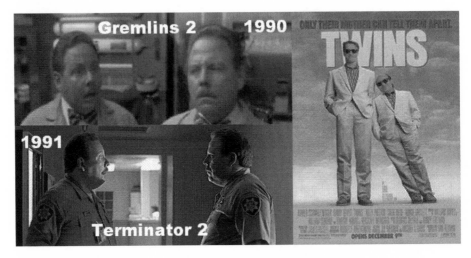

The soundtrack for "Gremlin 2" was hit of the pop group The Thompson Twins (yes, twins again), with the song "Bombers in the Sky". The original clip from 1989 featured the views of the Manhattan on the background and of course, twin towers. Unambiguous allusion on bombing and twin towers. The ingenuity of the creators of the film is truly admirable, but for a trained look the methods repeating over the many years are quite obvious.

Chapter VI History of the code 911

Before attempting to explain the meaning of one of the most basic codes in the movie industry, the media and other manifestations of popular culture, I will try to demonstrate its existence as clearly as possible. This code was discovered by researchers shortly after the events of September 11, 2001. The code was present in films, commercials, music videos, video games, media reports for dozens of years before the events of September 11, 2001. As you probably all remember, soon after these events appeared the so-called Movement for Truth, which called for a review of the official version of the events. In their view, some members of the US government were aware of the upcoming attacks on the World Trade Center and the Pentagon in far in advance but did nothing to prevent them. Others went even farther and accused entire US government of planning all these attacks for the speedy advancement of their political and economic agendas. The main accusations fell on President George W. Bush and Vice President Dick Cheney. Even the scandalous documentary "Fahrenheit 9/11" by American director Michael More, who openly accused George Bush of everything that happened was allowed to be shown on the movie screens legally though initially there were reported refusals of the large cinema chains to show it. Bottomline that Fahrenheit made its way to the large audience at last. People who criticized the US government did not receive a broad stage to express their criticism, but in some cases they, like Michael More and others, were allowed on the leading US TV channels. In contrast, observant people who did not engage in unfounded accusations of organized explosions in the WTC towers, the use of a "nano-termite", a "mini-nuclear explosion" under twin towers, "Tesla's weapons" and other unprovable things, were never allowed to the mainstream media, especially when it came to the occult side of the conspiracy. This component, based on a simple and intuitive mathematical processing of data, is much easier to identify, but it is not easy to explain to the average person, as this requires a massive body of knowledge in cryptography, religious and occult symbolism, the history of religions and other things that require the combination of several branches of knowledge in one person , technical and humanitarian. Understandably, for modern researchers this is a very rare combination. A researcher taking up against such a task, in order to get his message across, must first of all thoroughly understand the complexity of this task. Up to now, 80% of the critics of the official version of events 11/9, people pointing out its impossibility, being people with an engineering background, considering this version purely from a technical point of view. The rest are people who consider what happened only from the point of view of pragmatic political expediency. "Everything has been done to personally benefit the people affiliated with the government," "the interests of the oil-producing corporation," the occupation of Iraq and Afghanistan for the "regulation of oil prices," "the benefit of military-industrial complex," and other, very obvious things that nonetheless should not be discounted. But in all this there is something that almost no one takes into consideration- this is the occult component of any major political action. The only, and a fairly small group of researchers who give a proper importance to it, are researchers from among the fundamentalist Christians. Thanks to their good knowledge of the Bible, they are able to easily spot the codes embedded in media space, as their authors, basing them largely on the King James Bible (KJV), the Book of Revelations, apocryphal Christian books, the Jewish Torah and the Koran. In the codes there are also indications of the gods of other pantheons of antiquity, from the Sumerian-Babylonian, to the Ancient Greek, Celtic and Germanic. To a lesser extent there are codes based on Hindu and Buddhist beliefs, but they in any case, remain beyond the field of view of researchers from the Christian evangelical community. The drawback of such studies is that they try to give their interpretation of events only within narrow confessional frameworks, which is unacceptable for most critics outside of the framework of fundamentalist Christianity. Other researchers reduce everything to the notorious "Jewish conspiracy," blaming Israel and Jews, wholesale Freemasonry, which usually evokes opposition not only from the Jews themselves, but from all democratically minded readers, who are opposed to any kind of xenophobia.

There is a remarkable episode in history, illustrating the motives of George Bush to invade Iraq, which did not get to the most of the world's leading media, but still was allowed to make its way in to smaller outlets.

At the end of winter 2003, a few weeks before the outbreak of the war in Iraq, George W. Bush tried to persuade French president Jacques Chirac to participate in joint military action in Iraq. In the telephone conversation Bush had mentioned "forces of Gog and Magog at work". President Chirac had no clue what Bush was talking about, neither his office, so they turned for clarification to the Protestant Federation of France. Professor of Lausanne University in Switzerland Thomas Römer who was the country's foremost expert on Old Testament has prepared the summary. He explained who Gog and Magog were. They appear only twice in the Old Testament, once as a name, and once in a truly strange prophecy in the book of Ezekiel:

"And the word of the LORD came unto me, saying,

Son of man, set thy face against Gog, the land of Magog, the chief prince of Meshech and Tubal, and prophesy against him,

And say, Thus saith the Lord GOD; Behold, I am against thee, O Gog, the chief prince of Meshech and Tubal:

And I will turn thee back, and put hooks into thy jaws, and I will bring thee forth, and all thine army, horses and horsemen, all of them clothed with all sorts of armour, even a great company with bucklers and shields, all of them handling swords:

Persia, Ethiopia, and Libya with them; all of them with shield and helmet:

Gomer, and all his bands; the house of Togarmah of the north quarters, and all his bands: and many people with thee."

For the benefit of Chirac, Römer thoroughly penned a page on Gog and Magog: "They occur in Genesis, and in particular in two very obscure chapters in Ezekiel." That's a particularly baffling book, the theologian says: "It speculates on the future in a cryptic code that is intended for insiders."

The outlines are clear, though: "In chapters 38 and 39, a global army is formed to fight a final battle in Israel. That battle is ordained by God, in order to rid the world of His enemies, and thus herald in a new age." The axis of evil is composed mostly of nations to the north of Israel and led by Gog. The relation with Magog varies according to which particular translation you prefer. It could be "Gog and Magog," "Gog of Magog," "Gog, the land of Magog," or "Gog, prince of Magog." "These names are difficult to decode", says Römer, "just like Meshech and Tubal, also associated with the coalition, and equally enigmatic."

From that has been concluded, according to the biblical prophet Ezekiel, at the onset of the end of the world, Gog and Magog will come to Israel from Babylon (present-day Iraq).

For Gog and Magog - is the embodiment of the forces of Evil, and Babylon, located near Baghdad, which was ''restored'' by Saddam Hussein.

The Swiss theologian prefers to read Ezekiel in the context of its own time. "I think Ezekiel works along the lines of the apocalyptical prophecies in the book of Daniel, which refer to Antioch IV, a great contemporary adversary. Some researchers think Gog refers to Gygos, a king of Anatolia in the 7th century B.C." Römer thinks the obscure references in Ezekiel reflect the regional turmoil following Alexander the Great's foray into the Middle East: "The arrival of Hellenism was a culture shock. It probably propelled the locals to develop a chronology and to reflect on the succession of empires, the advent of new powers, and the emergence of a new era."

However, for those with a more literal understanding of the Bible, Ezekiel still reads like a relevant manual for the end times. For the book also describes the rebuilding of the Jewish Temple as a precondition for the return of the

Messiah. That site, on the Temple Mount in Jerusalem, is now occupied by the Dome of the Rock, one of Islam's holiest places. Try to build anything else in its place, and what follows will indeed closely resemble the Apocalypse.

Ezekiel is dear to many American Christians, as it provides a Biblical foundation for their proximity to Israel. "Like many others, Bush believes God will stand with Israel in the final showdown, and that Israel's enemies will therefore be in the camp of the Antichrist. He will support Israel no matter what."

In 1971, when still governor of California, Reagan said: "Ezekiel tells us that Gog, the nation that will lead all of the other powers of darkness against Israel, will come out of the north. Biblical scholars have been saying for generations that Gog must be Russia. What other powerful nation is to the north of Israel? None. But it didn't seem to make sense before the Russian revolution, when Russia was a Christian country. Now it does, now that Russia has become Communistic and atheistic, now that Russia has set itself against God. Now it fits the description of Gog perfectly."

In 2007 professor Romer has described the incident in the Lausanne University publication confirming other reports.

These are important illustrations to my thesis that political actions are not always governed by pragmatism which we assume for self- evident.

The was other important even which chronologically coincided with what is described in the account of professor Romer. In beginning of March 2003 several news outlets had reported about discovery of tomb of Gilgamesh, a legendary ruler of city of Uruk. Modern Iraq has its name deriving from this place. German-led expedition has discovered what is thought to be the entire city of Uruk - including, where the Euphrates once flowed, the last resting place of its famous King. The Epic of Gilgamesh - written by a Middle Eastern scholar 2,500 years before the birth of Christ - commemorated the life of the ruler of then magnificent city. Jorg Fassbinder, of the Bavarian department of Historical Monuments in Munich said the discovered tomb exactly fits description of Gilgamesh's burial according to a a set of inscribed clay tablets - Gilgamesh was described as having been buried under the Euphrates, in a tomb apparently constructed when the waters of the ancient river parted following his death. There were no further details revealed and then the discovery immediately faded from the news. As we all know the whole area was taken under control by US led coalition forces within weeks and we never heard anything back about this important discovery.

Roughly around same time surfaced the reports that more than half of the ancient exhibits were looted from the Iraqi National Museum in Baghdad. Later it was reported that the amount of thefts was greatly overstated, and that in fact no more than 1,000 exhibits out of 500,000 disappeared. Other reports claimed that more than 13,000 exhibits were missing. Who and how many exhibits were stolen is impossible to determine now, but it is clear that the occupation forces attached great importance to the ancient museum exhibits and archaeological finds, and I suspect that it has not been from humanistic considerations alone.

Let's return to President George Herbert Walker Bush or simply, Bush to the elder. On September 11, 1990, he pronounced his famous speech about a ''new world order'' before the joint session of the Congress dedicated to the crisis in the Persian Gulf and the federal budget deficit. Exactly 11 years later on September 11, 2001, twin towers will fall. The announcement of the military action of the Allies in the Persian Gulf against Iraq (the forces of Gog and Magog, about which Bush spoke to President J. Chirac) by President George W. Bush. took place also under the sign 911-16.01.1991

The key to US-China relations was the lifting of restrictions on exports to China by President George HW Bush, in a message to Congress on **11.9**.1992

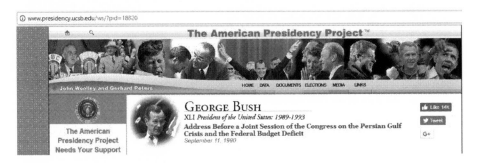

During his first and second inaugural speeches in 2000 and 2005, President George W. Bush partially quoted verses from the book of Ecclesiastes **9:11** and The Book of Revelations **9:11**:

Ecclesiastes 9:11King James Version (KJV)

11 "I returned, and saw under the sun, that the race is not to the swift, nor the battle to the strong, neither yet bread to the wise, nor yet riches to men of understanding, nor

yet favour to men of skill; but time and chance happeneth to them all."

George Bush while quoting these verses omitting from which book they are, instead he quotes them as part of John Page's letter to Thomas Jefferson:

"After the Declaration of Independence was signed, Virginia statesman John Page wrote to Thomas Jefferson: "We know the race is not to the swift nor the battle to the strong. Do you not think an angel rides in the whirlwind and directs this storm?"

Ecclesiastes is one of 24 books of the Tanakh or Hebrew Bible, where it is classified as one of the "Writings". Originally written c. 450-180 BCE, it is among the canonical Wisdom Books in the Old Testament of most denominations of Christianity. The title Ecclesiastes is a Latin transliteration of the Greek translation of the Hebrew Kohelet (meaning "Assembler", but traditionally translated as "Teacher" or "Preacher"), the pseudonym used by the author of the book.

The cryptic phrase about angel in the whirlwind comes from the poem by Joseph Adison "Marlborough at Blenheim" from the XVIII century.

So when an angel by divine command

With rising tempests shakes a guilty land,

Such as of late o'er pale Britannia past,

Calm and serene he drives the furious blast;

And, pleas'd th' Almighty's orders to perform,

Rides in the **whirlwind, and directs the storm**.

The poet was referring to the "old good Britain", which is indicated directly in the next stanza. Bush, therefore, had in mind the "guilty America".

Revelation 9:11 King James Version (KJV)

11 And they had a king over them, **which is the angel of the bottomless pit**, whose name in the Hebrew tongue is Abaddon, but in the Greek tongue hath his name Apollyon

In the second inaugural speech of George Bush, this eloquent phrase is also contained:

"When the Founders proclaimed a new order of the ages ... they acted according to the ancient aspiration that must be realized." In other words, the New World Order is again mentioned, only in a veiled, ancient form that stands on the back of the One dollar bill- Novus Ordo Seclorum (New Order of Ages literally)

There were no explanations made about the mysterious phrase about the angel directing storm from the White House's side, although it is clear that those who listened attentively to the speech clearly did not understand what it meant. The inauguration itself took place on January 20 (**20.1**), which gives you the key where to look for the answer. Book of Revelations **20.1** ''And I saw an angel come down from heaven, having the key of the bottomless pit and a great chain in his hand".

So, the key it is in a literal sense-one that unlocks the bottomless pit in which the Satan was locked for thousand years. In other words, proclamation of the Luciferian agenda right during inaugural speech.

I returned, and saw under the sun, that the race is not to the swift, nor the battle to the strong, neither yet bread to the wise, nor yet riches to men of understanding, nor yet favour to men of skill; but time and chance happeneth to them all.

And I saw an angel come down from heaven, having the key of the bottomless pit and a great chain in his hand.

Ecclesiastes **9:11** **Revelation** **20:1**

We know the Race is not to the swift nor the Battle to the Strong. Do you not think an Angel rides in the Whirlwind and directs this Storm? -George W. Bush, 1/20/2001

Another "coincidence" from this bizarre parade of oddities is a very website of the Saudi Bin Laden Construction Group which was established on 11.9.00 and preprogrammed to expire exactly on 11/09/01. Wired.com described this bizarre piece of history:

OSAMA FAMILY'S SUSPICIOUS SITE

FOR THE PRICE of registering a domain name, a 30-year-old Web designer from Los Angeles has bought a bizarre piece of Internet history.

On Oct. 27, Christopher Curry's company, Shrimpo.com, purchased a domain name that once belonged to the Saudi Binladin Group, the international construction conglomerate owned by the family of public enemy No. 1, Osama bin Laden.

What make Saudi-binladin-group.com so interesting is not just that it was once an official SBG website, but that it was

registered on Sept. 11, 2000, with a pre-set expiration date of Sept. 11, 2001, according to a "who is" search of the Internet domain registry VeriSign.
Efforts to reach SBG officials, through more than a half dozen phone calls and two e-mails to the firm's headquarters in Jeddah, Saudi Arabia, were unsuccessful.

Having the SBG domain registration expire on the day the United States was attacked is "a hell of a coincidence," said Charles Boncelet, a University of Delaware computer and information sciences professor, who is an expert on the field of steganography – the science of hiding information.

Law enforcement is already looking into whether the Sept. 11 attackers used seemingly innocuous websites or e-mails to transmit attack information using data embedded in audio or video files. The FBI will not comment about the SBG website expiration date being used as a signal to attackers – a signal that would mean the bin Laden family's public disavowal of their notorious 17th son, Osama, was merely a public relations ploy.

Regardless of whether the FBI is investigating the site, Curry purchased it and three other SBG domains.

At first, Curry – who recently entered the field of domain speculating – purchased the SBG domains thinking that he could sell them, at a handsome profit, with a portion of the proceeds going to the Red Cross disaster relief fund.

But Curry has decided that the domain name should not just be a portal to an empty site awaiting a quick sale. The site has received so many hits, as many as 13,000 per day, many from the Arab world, that Curry says he is going to turn the site into a full-fledged font of bin Laden info.

"I am going to use the site as an informational site about the bin Laden family," Curry said. "My friends are writing stories about the family history and we are going to have a feature called Binlinks, which are links to other sources of information about the family on the Web."

Click on the site now, and you will see a picture of Osama's head next to "bin Laden: From palace prince to cave dweller. Information about the world's most hated man."

There is also an ad for Liberty.Unites.org a charity. Curry said that in addition to serious information about the family and the terrorist, the site will "be a fun site, very interactive and a bit campy. There will be some animations, short little cartoon films."

The site will be fully operational by Nov. 15, he said. Shrimpo.com, which has produced websites for "everything from the adult industry to corporate work" has never attempted anything like this before, Curry said.

"I never realized how much time this would take," he said. "Of course, with the downfall of the IT industry, we have lots of time on our hands."

When he first put the site on line, Curry said he received hate mail from people wondering whether he was a terrorist and people upset that he would try to capitalize on the tragedy. While he hasn't heard from any law enforcement types or SBG representatives, Curry has discovered one drawback to operating saudi-binladin-group.com.

"I have gotten a lot of Arabic spam," he says. "Investment opportunities, you-can-make-money-now deals, those sorts of things."

Curiously Wired.com reported on this matter exactly on other 911 date-November 9(119).

As you can see, Osama bin Laden, Apollo (Apollo / Avvadon/Abbadon) and 911, written in words have the same gematria 11.

Nine One One	**WHOIS** Search Results
$\begin{pmatrix} \underline{n\ i\ n\ e} & \underline{o\ n\ e} & \underline{o\ n\ e} \\ 14\ 9\ 14\ 5 & 0 & 15\ 14\ 5 & 0 & 15\ 14\ 5 \end{pmatrix}$ in Simple Gematria Equals: **110**	Registrant: Saudi Binladin Group (SAUDI-BINLADIN-GROUP2-DOM) Prince Abdullah Street Jeddah, 21492 SA
Apollyon	Domain Name: SAUDI-BINLADIN-GROUP.COM
$\begin{pmatrix} \underline{a\ p\ o\ l\ l\ y\ o\ n} \\ 1\ 16\ 15\ 12\ 12\ 25\ 15\ 14 \end{pmatrix}$ in Simple Gematria Equals: **110**	Administrative Contact Technical Contact. Billing Lumsden, Philip (PLP239) philip@ARQ.CO.UK Arq Limited The Old Post Office George Street Bath, BA1 2EB UK 01224 312 391
Osama Bin Laden	
$\begin{pmatrix} \underline{o\ s\ a\ m\ a} & \underline{b\ i\ n} & \underline{l\ a\ d\ e\ n} \\ 15\ 19\ 1\ 13\ 1 & 0 & 2\ 9\ 14 & 0 & 12\ 1\ 4\ 5\ 14 \end{pmatrix}$ in Simple Gematria Equals: **110**	Record last updated on 11-Sep-2000 Record expires on 11-Sep-2001 Record created on 11-Sep-2000 Database last updated on 4-Oct-2001 16:34:00 EDT

مجموعة بن لادن السعودية

SAUDI BINLADIN GROUP

ARCHITECTURE & BUILDING CONSTRUCTION DIVISION

The main lobbyist for the construction of the twin towers of the WTC was David Rockefeller and his brother Nelson, then governor of New York. The Rockefeller family has already tried to build on its land the highest hotel in the world, even commissioned for the project the most famous architect of the early XX century Antonio Gaudi. For some reason, John D. Rockefeller found this project too expensive and abandoned the idea. About its existence we've learned only recently, when sketches of the hotel were found. The name of the customer was not reported, but by indirect indications it is clear, that it could only be him. His sons continued work of his father and during their life time the twin towers were built. On a rare photograph from the cover of Newsweek magazine on April 3, 1967, David Rockefeller is depicted with a wrist watch, the hands of which are shown on the 9 and 11. Every year on November 29 (29.11) in front of the Rockefeller Center in New York huge Christmas tree is lit. The lighting ceremony, for 86 consecutive years begins exactly at 8:55. Look at the analog clock and you will realize that 8:55 is no other than 911.

8:55

Naturally, by "chance", twin towers were built each 110
floors high, which is completely coincides with the Nine
One One gematria of 110, gematria of the name of the
Rockefeller-110, initiator of the project, as well as Osama
bin Laden, his official, so to speak, finalizer. To top it off,
Rockefeller managed to survive to 101, and in this case this
might be also manipulation with numbers in the media. In
numerology you may reduce 110 to 11 so is 101.

Rockefeller in English Gematria Equals: **660** (r o c k e f e l l e r / 108 90 18 66 30 36 30 72 72 30 108)

Rockefeller in Simple Gematria Equals: **110** (r o ck efel l er / 18 15 3 11 5 6 5 12 12 5 18)

In his book "Memoirs", which David Rockefeller published
in 2000 on page 405 he boldly admits: "Some even
believe we [Rockefeller family] are part of a secret cabal
working against the best interests of the United States,
characterizing my family and me as 'internationalists' and
of conspiring with others around the world to build a more
integrated global political and economic structure - One
World, if you will. If that's the charge, I stand guilty, and I
am proud of it."

Here is another interesting quote:

"We are grateful to The Washington Post, The New York
Times, Time Magazine and other great publications whose

directors have attended our meetings and respected their promises of discretion for almost forty years. It would have been impossible for us to develop our plan for the world if we had been subject to the bright lights of publicity during those years. But, the work is now much more sophisticated and prepared to march towards a World Government. The supranational sovereignty of an intellectual elite and world bankers is surely preferable to the national auto-determination practiced in past centuries." David Rockefeller to Trilateral Commission in 1991

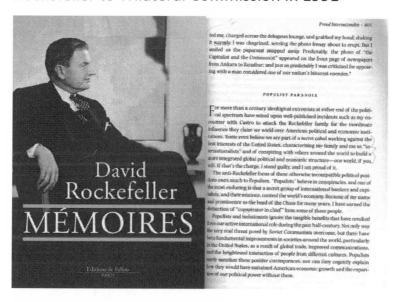

As I already mentioned above, the book of the Apocalypse, Revelation of John the Divine is one of the most widely used books of the New Testaments for coding the secret messages. The author of the controversial book "The Caesar's Messiah. The Roman conspiracy of the invention of Jesus", Joseph Atwill pointed out the method of interpretation of the four main Gospels. According to Atwill you need to read them always in the context of the Old Testament, as well as using Josephus' Favius books -

Judean war and Antiquities of the Jews. He is convinced that Josephus is the original author at least one of New Testament versions. Thus, all the parables in them must be interpreted through chronologically similar events described in aforementioned books of Josephus. I'm not talking about the very essence of the author's statements concerning person of Christ, whose "invention" Atwill ascribes to Roman emperor Vespasian and his son Titus. He hypothesized that the real authors of the Gospels were Roman emperors of the Flavian clan with the help of Josephus. The subject of the Atwill's book is very controversial but nevertheless I consider his recommendation of using typology extremely useful for breaking the codes. He pointed out that ancient tradition in Jewish literature to consisted of non-literal, typological references to earlier books that indicated, without naming names to similar characters, events and parables in other books. Typology in Christian theology and biblical exegesis is a doctrine or theory relating to the relation of the Old Testament to the New Testament. Events, personalities or statements in the Old Testament are considered as types that are preceded or replaced by the antitypes, events or aspects of Christ or his revelations described in the New Testament. For example, Jonah can be considered as a type of Christ because he came out of the belly of a fish and, as it turned out, rose after death. In the most complete version of the theory of typology, the whole purpose of the Old Testament is viewed as simply providing types for Christ, a prototype or execution. In the same way, the essence of political speeches or the meaning of films becomes clear only when you understand in combination with which other document, book or film you have to interpret the content. To put it simply, imagine that you agreed with the author of the cipher to use the key to it, contained in a certain book, on a certain page. People for a cipher is intended simply have a serious set of knowledge that helps them without any reference literature to guess where to look for the key to the cipher. Films, musical videos and texts are related by code words, through which they (or parts of them) can, in many different ways, explicitly or implicitly refer to each other. In other words, if the film "Back to the Future" is mentioned directly or indirectly in "Donnie Darko", then there will be a key to the cipher, or at least one of them.

The birthday of George Walker Bush-July 6, 1946. In fact, George W. Bush and the twin towers of the WTC were born on the same day- " The Governor of New York elects a board of directors for the construction of the World Trade Center ". New York Times for July 6, 1946. "The Dewey Picks Board for Trade Center." The New York Times, July 6, 1946. Thus, the WTC project was born simultaneously with George W. Bush and was destroyed under his presidency.

One of the first Hollywood films containing the code 911 was released in 1947, long before the twin towers were even built in 1973. The film is titled "I'll be yours" - 'I' '- the ninth letter of the English alphabet and two' 'll' 'look like' '11' '. The main character of the film **George W. Prescott**. The main female character is Louise JingleBUSHer. Grandfather of George W. Bush was named Prescott Bush.

The inscription on the window of George Prescott's office is shown in such a way that PREScott can be read as a "president". All this can be called a "cherry picking" if not for combination of codes, which over the years have been identified in hundreds of films.

This is the beginning of movie " Pretty Woman ", released 23.3.90 with a length of 119 minutes (911)

" Meteor ", 10/19/79 (911), twin towers, explosion, 911

"L.A Confidential" 14.5.97 -911 on the clock

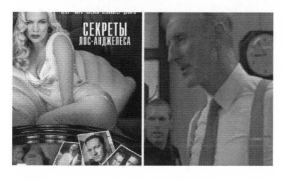

"Monsters Inc" 28.10.01, 911 on the clock

"The 13th floor" 28.5.1999 911 on the clock

''The Paper'' 18.03.1994 911 on the watch

''The Crow'' 5.11.1994 ,911 on the clock and on the display of the detonator

Pop group Erasure (demolition, destruction) The clip was released on November 27, 1989 (2 + 7 = 9 November = 11th month)

From the date of the release of the clip "You surround me" to 11.09.01 will be **11** years and **9** months. In the frame constantly flashing twin towers, twice the sign of Baphomet (horned hand) is shown, while towers appear on the background.

" You gotta **shake me down"**

" Oh **take me down** to the very root of my soul"

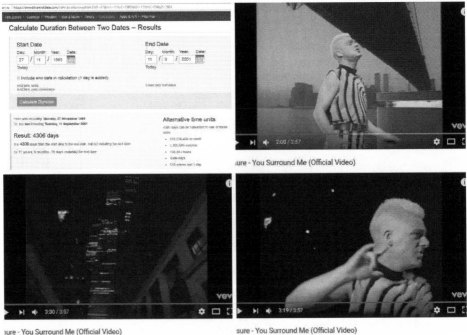

ure - You Surround Me (Official Video)

;ure - You Surround Me (Official Video)   sure - You Surround Me (Official Video)

One of the first Hollywood movies that I know of containing the code 911- "Deluge" was released in August 18, 19**33**. New York is disappearing under the tidal waves, towers resembling the World Trade Center are crumbling under the power of huge waves. The film opens with a quote from Genesis **9:11** " And I will establish my covenant with you, neither shall all flesh be cut off any more by the waters of a flood; neither shall there any more be a flood to destroy the earth." 1973 is a year of the opening of the twin towers of the World Trade Center which fell on the Jewish year **5733**.

Exactly such an end to New York that is predicted by mysterious bas-reliefs on the columns of the strangest Episcopal Cathedral of St. John the Divine at the corner of Amsterdam Avenue and 112th Street in New York. The columns depict scenes of absorption by waves of twin towers and other buildings of the city. Outside the cathedral there are statues of gloomy, one-eyed creatures. On one of the bas-reliefs is clearly referencing to the birth of the Antichrist. The other depicts the Kabbalistic Tree of Life (10 Sephiroth), which is quite surprising to see on the Christian church. Inside, next to the altar, there is a large Jewish seven branched candlestick-Menorah. The cathedral is located in New York's Morningside Heights area. The cathedral (was built in honor of Saint John the Divine). As of February 2018, the construction of the cathedral is still incomplete. The cathedral's area is 11,240 m², the volume is 476,350 m³, length is 183.2 m. Thus, the cathedral is the largest Anglican cathedral in the world.

The construction of the cathedral started on December 27, 1892 It was planned in Byzantine-Romanesque style, but in 1911 the style was changed to a new Gothic. Who is the author of strange bas-reliefs, their significance, as well as the accurate year of their completion remains unknown.

Advertising of the Pakistan International Airways in French magazine Le Point from 1979

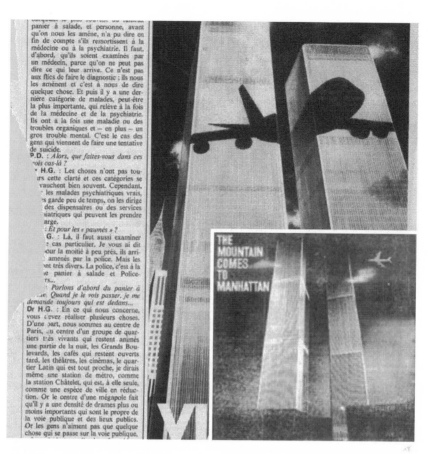

There are also cases that go beyond the usual methods of coding. The following case is perhaps the most unusual of all analyzed by me. In 1991, Jean-Charles Wall, now living in Montpellier, bought an ordinary Afghan carpet with an unusual design.

It all started in Paris, on the same day in May 1991, the most common morning. Wall was looking for a carpet for his little daughter. He spotted a tiny shop where hundreds of carpets were heaped up. At first glance, nothing attracted his attention. When he was ready to turn around and leave the shop, he sees behind a box in a corner, a pile where about ten carpets of the coveted blue were folded.

He asks the shopkeeper, so that they can be more closely examined. Carpets amaze him with a variety of patterns and bright colors. He discusses the price with a young salesman who replaced his boss during the lunch break. The purchase is for 1,300 francs, which he pays in cash. Jean-Charles Wall goes home and arranges his acquisition in the middle of his daughter's room, which was delighted with the gift.

In 1998, Jean-Charles moved to Montpellier and found work in the field of interior design. He became the designer of two apartments with a terrace and a swimming pool on the roof, in the area of Rives-du-les. On September 11, 2001, Wall works in his workshop when news cast attracts attention on television: two aircraft have just crashed into the Twin Towers of the World Trade Center in the heart of Manhattan. At first he does not catch the connection. In the middle of the night, he wakes up in anxiety and realizes that the motives of the carpet bought ten years ago have much in common with the images he sees on television. It is from this moment on, the designer begins to be fascinated with the history of the origin of this carpet.

He contacts Philippe Emir, an oriental carpet expert, and two scientists from the University of Canberra, Australia, who have dedicated their research to war rugs (the so-called Afghan carpets with military themes). Several elements confirm that his property is identical to the reproduction of the Brooklyn Bridge, a bridge that adjoins Manhattan, which suffered from the attacks of 11 September. The carpet is 133 cm long and 86 cm wide and full of symbols. Full decoding of the carpet takes more than six years. Various scientific expertise and personal research will lead to some very worrying end results: his daughter's former playground is an Afghan war, a propaganda carpet made in the Balochistan region in 1369 by the Afghan calendar, corresponding to the period of March 21, 1990, until March 21, 1991 according to the results radiocarbon analysis. These dates coincide with the Iraq-Kuwait war. In addition, the carpet depicts six events. The carpet depicts 10 aircraft over New York. According to the report of the US investigative bodies, "The terrorist scenario, implemented in the USA on September 11, 2001, began to be developed back in 1996. About this Khalid Sheikh Mohammed confessed US intelligence services during interrogations.

Considered the closest associate of Al-Qaeda leader Osama bin Laden and one of the organizers of the terrorist attacks in New York and Washington, Khalid Sheikh Mohammed was captured in Rawalpindi by Pakistani and US intelligence agencies in March this year.

Khalid Sheikh Mohammed admitted that the terrorist attacks were planned by him and Osama bin Laden. He claims that he and Osama bin Laden planned on September 11, 2001, "more large-scale terrorist attacks." According to the original plan, it was planned to hijack ten passenger aircraft on both coasts of the US and use them as "cruise missiles." "An exact analysis also identifies 96 Ishtar stars along the rim of the carpet, the goddess of revenge in the context. The interpreting experts that note that those are of particular importance in the Afghan tradition carpet weaving. On the carpet 4 inscriptions in several local languages, two of them above the bridge and two under it. In place of the Northern Tower of the WTC, the inscription is "this special work". The inscription on the site of the South Tower is the "goal of wealth" or "sign of luck." A cryptic inscription under the bridge, as if reflected in water means "cleansing" or "erasing".

So, the most unusual about this carpet that it displays a prior knowledge on the part of some unknown Afghan carpet maker or the person who commissioned this carpet. All this is in stark contrast with the Hollywood production where you may at least suppose how such a sensitive knowledge might have been proliferated.

Philips TV ad from 1996. Aircraft on the background of twin towers. It is noteworthy that the gematria of the company's name is 44, that is, as in the Tribute in Light show on Zero Ground, 44 searchlights per tower, 88 in total.

Comic book Spiderman 1991

The Simpsons animated series are famous for its so-called "predictions". Events 11.09.2001 is one of the themes that has repeatedly appeared in various episodes of the cartoon, since the mid-1990s. The cartoon characters are depicted on the background of figures 9 and 11, then against the backdrop of one of the twin towers, like Homer Simpson with the car full money that broke down right under one of the towers. In another episode, the towers are enveloped in the smoke and fire.

The number of cartoons, comic books, promotional items, posters, video games with hints of the destruction of the twin towers well before 11.9.01 is just off scale. The pages of this book are not enough to illustrate all the information

I and other researchers have collected. On the collage below there are some comic books published before the construction of the twin towers of the WTC.

Especially eloquent is the cover of Michael Jackson's 1997 album "Blood on the Dance Floor," where Michael's legs are obscuring invisible towers, behind him a cloud of ashes rising above New York, exactly as it will happen on September 11, 2001, when the towers collapsed.Michael's hands are in the position of hour and minute hands on 9 and 11.

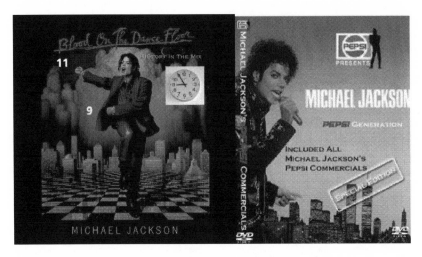

Another prior to 911 Michael Jackson's Pepsi Generation ad where he points his finger in direction of twin towers.

One of the notable films that showed the collapse of the twin towers was the "Time Machine" based on the novel penned by GH Wells. It is noteworthy that Wells published in 1940 a book titled "New World Order". Prior to that, he had already published the book "The Open Conspiracy" in 1928. The film begins with the falling ashes, as was seen on the television screen after crumbling of twin towers of the WTC on September 11, 2001. The 41-year-old Alan Young, born on 1**9.11**.1919 (911), was selected for one of the main roles.

The first journey to the future took place in August 17, 1966 (August 4, according to the Julian calendar) - the construction of the twin towers of the WTC will begin the next day.

Pay attention to the picture of the crumbling world accompanied by the falling ashes. Just to the left of the center, silhouettes of twin towers appear (the construction of which will begin only 6 years after the film was released in 1960). On the next frame the towers disappear. 41 years

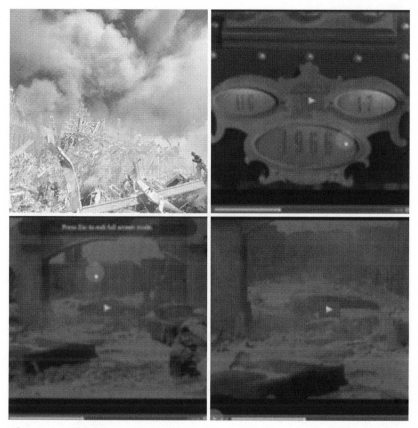

after the film's release, on 11.9.01 they will disappear in reality. As usual for all the films associated with time travel it comes with the code 88. First time travel date was August 18 (1 + 7 and 8).

I conclude this presentation with a collage with a dozen of well-known Hollywood films containing hints to the events of September 11, 2001 long before them. The list can be continued indefinitely, since I have several hundreds of such examples at my disposal.

Passport with 911 date from "Matrix" 1999

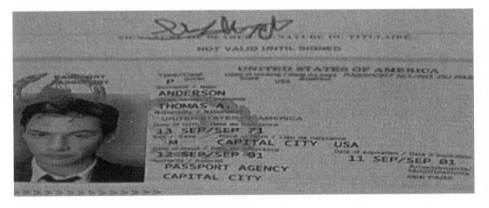

Above screenshot from "Armageddon" 1998 and below
actual TV footage of burning twin towers on 911.

Chapter VII Esoteric Origins of the Code 911

I hope that after such vast quantity of examples you became convinced that 911 code is not a product of apophenia, but really embedded in modern media space and even architecture. It remains to be seen the exact significance of the code beyond of what lies on the surface-the predictions of Twin Towers demolition in New York. One unique archeological find will help us to find out.

The sailboat "La Belle" (Beauty), which sunk in 1686, was discovered in 1995 in the Gulf of Mexico off the coast of Texas. "La Belle" was part of the expedition of Cavelier de la Salle in 1684.

French "La Belle" is one of the most significant archaeological finds in the history of Texas. It was on this ship that the researcher René-Robert Cavelier Sieur de la Salle, set off down the Mississippi River in 1684 to claim the new territories for king of France. The ship, instead went to the Gulf of Matagorda, where it sank in 1686. He was discovered 300 years later in 1995. La Belle is now at the center of the exhibition on the ground floor of Bullock museum, which was specially built around the remains of a sailboat in order to avoid damage to exhibits during transportation. The most valuable find on the sailboat for my search of the 911 code origins, were a lot of copper and bronze rings, which the priests of the Jesuits order (Society of Jesus) brought with them. In total, about 1500 rings of 16 different designs were found, but to make a point only those that are shown below are of interest. IXXI is 911 in Roman numerals. What connection did the Jesuit fathers have to a relatively young symbol, the history of which I was able to trace at that time only from the beginning of the twentieth century? It was difficult for me to imagine that the symbol could have been known at least in the XVII century.

At the moment, the September 11, 2001 memorial in New York contains exhibits with a similar symbol.

The works of the famous artist Isabel Dufresne IXXI Ultraviolet which she calls " the symbol of the New Era ".

Official historians of Christian symbolism explain that in fact, the IXXI is not about the Roman numerals 9 and 11, but about the intersecting letters M and A, which is an anagram for "Under the auspices of Mary." The emblem and motto served as a symbol of the Society of Priests of Saint Sulpicius, founded in 1642 by the French priest Jean-Jacques Olier. Theoretically, this does not contradict my version, for Virgin Mary and Mary Magdalene are also an important part of the code, which I will demonstrate later in my following book. However, as for the rings, they were discovered with different designs, one of which really resembles an anagram of Sulpicians, but others, no doubt show the Roman numerals IX and XI.

Works of Isabelle Dufresne at 9/11 memorial in New York with IXXI symbols

The church of Saint Sulpicius in Paris was mentioned in such different works as "Twenty Thousand Leagues Under the Sea" by Jules Verne and what is especially interesting is the "Da Vinci Code" by Dan Brown. Latter, in addition to popularizing ancient codes and ciphers in his works used those secretly in his book. In first edition of "Da Vinci Code" Dan Brown has elegantly sent the brothers Masons the encrypted message, in which he made it clear that he is one of them. This was done in a style that was in harmony with the plot of the book itself, which contained the key phrase. I cannot say about all the editions, but in the first edition of the hardcover the message was there. If you open the first pages of the book, you will see that some letters are highlighted in a font, fatter than others. If you collect all these letters in the order they are placed, they will add up in the phrase "O Lord, my God! Is there no help for the widow's son?"

This ritual phrase was described by the former Mason, Captain William Morgan in his 1826 book.

Morgan's book was called "Explanation of Freemasonry by one of the brotherhood dedicated to the subject for 30 years"; in it the author exposed the essence and methods of Masonry. In 1827 book was self-published in Batavia, New York. Dogma of Freemasonry states that anyone who discloses the secrets of the Order will be punished. After a while, several Masons kidnapped and killed Captain Morgan, despite of having a large family.

The scandal caused a strong public outcry and led to the fact that over 45,000 of the 50,000 Masons in the United States "withdrew from the brotherhood." On September thirteenth, 1882, a column was erected in Batavia in honor of William Morgan, on which you can read the description of these events.

In 1848 Henry Valance confessed that Morgan was killed by drowning. The rope tied around the waist was tied with stones weighing more than the body. Then the kidnappers dropped him into Niagara, having heard the crying and pleading for the preservation of life. Clearly the Masonic murder caused a wide public response. A few years later, former Masons working at the state government level, established a trust fund to compensate Morgan's wife and children for their loss.

According to testimonies, the founder of the Mormon Church, Joseph Smith was killed by a mob, among whom were Freemasons, despite the fact that he also uttered the code phrase " O Lord, God, is there no help for the widow's son? " He raised his hands, according to the ritual of the call for deliverance. Nevertheless, he was killed, since he included in Mormon worship a Masonic ritual that was not subject to disclosure.

Langdon and Neveu find themselves matching wits with a faceless powerbroker who appears to anticipate their every move. Unless they can decipher the labyrinthine puzzle, the Priory's secret—and an explosive ancient truth—will be lost forever.

Breaking the mold of traditional suspense novels, *The Da Vinci Code* is simultaneously lightning-paced, intelligent, and intricately layered with remarkable research and detail. From the opening pages to the unpredictable and stunning conclusion, bestselling author Dan Brown proves himself a master storyteller

MASONRY

– BY –

ONE OF THE FRATERNITY

Who has devoted Thirty Years to the Subject.

"God said, Let there be Light, and there was Light."

Copyright Secured.

Printed for the Proprietor, 1827.

CAPT. WM. MORGAN'S

EXPOSITION OF

FREEMASONRY

However, the 911 code has even more ancient history. In Jewish history, Tisha B'Av (9th Av) is celebrated as the day of mourning for the greatest tragedies in the history of the Jewish people-the destruction of the First Temple of Solomon by the Babylonians and the Second Temple of Herod by the Romans. Both these events occurred on the 9th Av, 586 BC. e and 9 Av 3828 (70) CE. In the Jewish lunar religious calendar, 9th Av usually falls on June-July according to the Gregorian calendar. The lunar calendar fluctuates relative to the dates of the Gregorian calendar. The month of Av is the 5th on the account of the Jewish lunar calendar. The count is starting from the month of Nisan, as prescribed in the Torah. However, if we count starting from the new year of Rosh Hashanah, which falls on the month of Tishrei, as we do in Gregorian calendar counting from January 1st, then Av becomes the 11th month. Thus, the tragedies of the 9th day of the month of Av are in fact occurred on the 11th month of the year. Numerologically, Tisha B'Av has a value of 911 in Jewish gematria using Latin letters. I do not think there is anything mystical about this, and for this reason: In 1611, the so-called Bible of King James(KJV) came out in England, which for more than a year was edited by one of the greatest minds of the time, Francis Bacon. He is considered by some scholars as the architect of modern English language, which he structured to strictly correspond to gematria, just as it was with Hebrew and Greek languages. It is possible that even the year the Bible was released -1611, was not accidental. It is known that most of the priests of that time branded this publication as "satanic" and continued to use the so-called Geneva Bible of 1560 edition, which served as the main Bible for English protestants in the 16th century. I will dwell on this in more detail later, but now we will try to track the presence of 9 Awa in history after the destruction of the First and Second Temples.

It is also important that September 11 is a new year in the Ethiopian and Coptic calendars. Some Christian denominations believe that September 11 was the real birthday of Christ, and not a pagan holiday on December

25, which later the Catholic Church will use to celebrate Christmas. The following list of events that are described as they had happened on 9 Av in the Bible. Further, the remaining majority of events are quite verifiable, as they were described in historical chronicles. The list is quite impressive:

According to the Mishnah (Taanit 4:6), five specific events occurred on the ninth of Av that warrant fasting:

The Twelve Spies sent by Moses to observe the land of Canaan returned from their mission. Only two of the spies, Joshua and Caleb, brought a positive report, while the others spoke disparagingly about the land. The majority report caused the Children of Israel to cry, panic and despair of ever entering the "Promised Land". For this, they were punished by God that their generation would not enter the land. Because of the Israelites' lack of faith, God decreed that for all generations this date would become a day of crying and misfortune for their descendants. (See Numbers 13; Numbers 14).

The First Temple built by King Solomon and the Kingdom of Judah destroyed by the Babylonians led by Nebuchadnezzar in 587 BCE (Anno Mundi [AM] 3175) after a two-year siege and the Judeans were sent into the Babylonian exile. According to the Talmud in tractate Ta'anit, the actual destruction of the First Temple began on the Ninth of Av and the Temple continued to burn throughout the Tenth of Av.

The Second Temple built by Ezra and Nehemiah was destroyed by the Romans in August 70 CE (AM 3830), scattering the people of Judea and commencing the Jewish exile from the Holy Land that continues to this day.

The Romans subsequently crushed Bar Kokhba's revolt and destroyed the city of Betar, killing over 500,000 Jewish civilians (approximately 580,000) on August 4, 135 CE (Av 9, AM 3895).

Following the Bar Kokhba revolt, Roman commander Turnus Rufus plowed the site of the Temple in Jerusalem and the surrounding area, in 135 CE.

Note: Due to a two-year difference within the Hebrew calendar, the years in which the First and Second Temple were destroyed have been disputed. Though it has been accepted by most historians to refer to the most modern interpretation of the Calendar (which corresponds to the Roman siege of Jerusalem in 70 CE.)

Over time, Tisha B'Av has come to be a Jewish day of mourning, not only for these events, but also for later tragedies. Regardless of the exact dates of these events, for many Jews, Tisha B'Av is the designated day of mourning for them, and these themes are reflected in liturgy composed for this day.

Other calamities associated with Tisha B'Av:

The First Crusade officially commenced on August 15, 1096 (Av 24, AM 4856), killing 10,000 Jews in its first month and destroying Jewish communities in France and the Rhineland.

The Jews were expelled from England on July 18, 1290 (Av 9, AM 5050). The Jews were expelled from France on July 22, 1306 (Av 10, AM 5066).

The Jews were expelled from Spain on July 31, 1492 (Av 7, AM 5252).

Germany entered World War I on August 1–2, 1914 (Av 9–10, AM 5674), which caused massive upheaval in European Jewry and whose aftermath led to the Holocaust.

On August 2, 1941 (Av 9, AM 5701), SS commander Heinrich Himmler formally received approval from the Nazi Party for "The Final Solution." As a result, the Holocaust began during which almost one third of the world's Jewish population perished.

On July 23, 1942 (Av 9, AM 5702), began the mass deportation of Jews from the Warsaw Ghetto, en route to Treblinka.

Most religious communities use Tisha B'Av to mourn the 6,000,000 Jews who perished in the Holocaust, including special kinnot composed for this purpose (see the main kinnot article) (in addition to, or instead of, the secular Holocaust Memorial Days.)

On the 10th of Av the following events took place:

AMIA bombing of the Jewish community center in Buenos Aires, killing 85 and injuring 300 on 18 July 1994; 10 Av, AM 5754

The Israeli disengagement from Gaza starts in the Gaza Strip, expelling 8000 Jews who lived in Gush Katif; 15 August 2005; 10 Av, 5765.

My hypothesis from the eschatological point of view is that
adherents of secret societies from the Knights Templar to
modern Masons (of course, it's not about ordinary
members) see the hand of God in such regularity of events,
but not in its biblical interpretation. In the Masonic
interpretation, god is not the God of the Bible, but Lucifer
(Satan), who is also Prometheus, who brings light and
enlightenment to people. Main point of masonic
interpretation of the enlightenment is that God of the
Bible according to their cosmology, has been preventing
the proliferation of knowledge amongst humans unlike the
Serpent(Satan/Lucifer) was giving the carnal knowledge to
Adam and Eve in the Garden of Eden. This doctrine you
can find in Helen Blavatsky's "The Secret Doctrine", as well
as the greatest theorist of the Masonic dogma Albert Pike
in "Morals and Dogma". "Lucifer represents.. Life..
Thought.. Progress.. Civilization.. Liberty.. Independence..
Lucifer is the Logos.. the Serpent, the Savior." pages 171,
225, 255 (Volume II) The secret Doctrine, HP Blavatsky "It
is Satan who is the God of our planet and the only God."
pages 215, 216, 220, 245, 255, 533.

"The Celestial Virgin which thus becomes the Mother of
Gods and Devils at one and the same time; for she is the

ever-loving beneficent Deity...but in antiquity and reality Lucifer or Luciferius is the name. Lucifer is divine and terrestrial Light, 'the Holy Ghost' and 'Satan' at one and the same time." page 539 Beginning in the early to mid-Nineteenth Century, and with the incorporation of Eastern mystical concepts into the existing traditions, the Western Mystery Tradition experienced a major divergence between the esoteric Hermetic rites of the Masonic and Rosicrucian traditions, and the Theosophical schools (with the major divergence occurring during the life of Madame Blavatsky) that came to be grouped under the general rubric of New Age spirituality.

"Lucifer, the Light-Bearer! Strange and mysterious name to give to the Spirit of Darkness! Lucifer, the Son of the Morning! Is it he who bears the light, and with its splendors intolerable blinds feeble, sensual or selfish Souls? Doubt it not!"

Albert Pike, Morals and Dogma of the Ancient and Accepted Scottish Rite of Freemasonry Prepared for the Supreme Council of the Thirty-Third Degree, for the Southern Jurisdiction of the United States, and Published by Its Authority (Richmond, Virginia: L.H. Jenkins, 1871, Reprinted 1944): 321.

The apostle Paul tells us that Satan masquerades as an angel of light: "And no marvel; for Satan himself is transformed into an angel of light (2 Corinthians 11:14)". In numerous New Age literature including the works of Theosophical society there are plenty of apologist for Albert Pike and Helena Blavatsky playing the card of Leo

Taxil's anti-masonic hoax, constantly downplaying these authentic quotes calling it "bogus Luciferian doctrine".

By the way, Blavatsky's "Secret Doctrine" was favorite book of Adolf Hitler, and it was because of her that the Nazis chose the swastika as their symbol. The authors of the "911 project" really chose 9 Av as a symbol of the destruction of the old Temple (old covenant) and construction of the "new", but not according to the biblical covenant, but as Satan does in the book of Revelations of John the Divine-taunting and mocking God, challenging him. Twin towers were purposely built to be destroyed at some point, because they represented the old world, the old Temple, the destruction of which was supposed to symbolize the beginning of the New World Order (Novus Ordo Seclorum as it states on the back of one-dollar bill). Twin Towers, each of which was to represent **23** pairs of chromosomes (a human chromosome set), which would later merge into one **46** chromosomal hybrid, as set forth in Daniel's prophecy and what is described in the apocryphal book of Enoch, which warned against mixing with the fallen angels (Book of Enock chapter XII). A new hybrid, the New World Order, the new " temple " represents a new tower Freedom Tower (One World Trade Center), which arose on the site of the ruins of twin towers. Do you think that such a concept is pulled out of thin air? Then look at the cover of Time magazine from March 3, 2003 (23). Is it accidental that President George W. Bush, in his televised speech on the evening of September 11, 2001, read exactly Psalm 23? 23 is an interesting number by itself, producing 0.**666** when dividing 2 by 3. Did President Obama read the **46** Psalms accidentally at a ceremony commemorating the 10th anniversary of the events of September 11, on 11.09.11? The construction of the Second Temple by Herod the Great continued for 46 years.

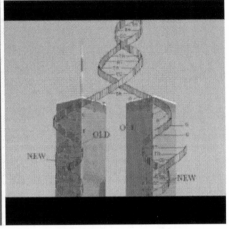

The Third Temple is not the one that should be built only after the return of the Messiah to Jerusalem, but the one that the imitators have already built in New York in the form of the Freedom Tower that stands now on the site of the fallen twin towers. This same "temple", on one of the beams of which President Obama, personally put the sign **"666"**, in the form of a string of letters "WWW", which have the sixth ordinal number in the Hebrew alphabet. "We remember, We rebuild, We come back stronger". The same magic phrase Obama will say a year later, on November 3, 2012 after the hurricane Sandy, replacing the word "remember" with "recover". It is noteworthy that in the Bible compiled under King James (KJV), in England in 1611, **Psalm 46** was on **666**th page. The total height of all buildings of the original WTC was 6660 feet. What

President Obama said twice is nothing else than quote from Isaiah 9:10 and the fulfillment of his prophecy. "The bricks fell - we will build from the hewn stone, the **sycamore** trees are cut down - we will replace them with cedar." It would seem on surface there is no connection, but twin towers of the WTC obviously symbolized the "bricks", and the new Freedom Tower-symbolic hewn, polished stones. It was particularly polished stone that was solemnly laid on 4.07.04 in the foundation of the new Freedom Tower. The remains of the **sycamore**, which used to grow at the WTC grounds in New York until September 11, 2001, are on display, even though there is not much left of it. Planted in 2003, the cedar came to replace the burned on 11.9.01 sycamore, as it was supposed to fulfill the prophecy of Isaiah. The bottom line-the prophecy was either self-fulfilling, or rather fulfilled "manually".

Yod	Tet	Chet	Zayin	Vav	He	Dalet	Gimel	Bet	Alef
(Y)	(T)	(Ch)	(Z)	(V/W)	(H)	(D)	(G)	(B/V)	(silent)
10	9	8	7	6	5	4	3	2	1

Ayin	Samech	Nun	Nun	Mem	Mem	Lamed	Khaf	Kaf
(silent)	(S)	(N)	(N)	(M)	(M)	(L)	(Kh)	(K/Kh)
70	60		50		40	30		20

Tav	Shin	Resh	Qof	Tsadeh	Tsadeh	Feh	Peh
(T)	(Sh/S)	(R)	(Q)	(Ts)	(Ts)	(F)	(P/F)
400	300	200	100		90		80

Remains of the sycamore from the Ground Zero, the new cedar, polished cornerstone of Freedom Tower and president Obama inscribing the new WTC beam with "WWW"

The authors of the Project 911 managed to link the original and current WTC with all occult concepts, from ancient Egypt to Freemasonry, and this track can be found not only in the architecture or mathematics of the project, especially after having studied the well-kept track record of the chief architect of the twin towers Minoru Yamasaki.

An American architect of Japanese origin, Minoru Yamasaki, not only symbolically portrayed the Nile and the pyramids of Giza in the WTC complex, but also combined Islamic designs in the design of the twin towers with hints to the sacred stone of the Kaaba in Mecca, the constellation of Orion and many other esoteric concepts. All this information is available in open sources to anyone who is interested in the architectural side of the Twin Towers project. Monument representing Egyptian pyramids for a long time stood on the territory of the WTC complex. Minoru Yamasaki was the author of many projects in Saudi Arabia, from the airport in Dhahran to the Monetary authority head office of Saudi Arabia, was the favorite architect of the royal family of Saud. He was so loaded with orders from them that he was not even physically able to take on all these projects. Let me remind you that the whole complex around the Kaaba in Mecca was built by the construction firm of Mohammed bin Laden, the father of the notorious Osama. Yamasaki received the World Trade Center commission the year after the Dhahran Airport was completed. Yamasaki described its plaza as "a mecca, a great relief from the narrow streets and sidewalks of the surrounding Wall Street area." True to his word, Yamasaki replicated the plan of Mecca's courtyard by creating a vast delineated square, isolated from the city's bustle by low colonnaded structures and capped by two enormous, perfectly square towers—minarets, really. Yamasaki's courtyard mimicked Mecca's assemblage of holy sites—the Kaaba (a cube) containing the sacred stone, what some believe is the burial site of Hagar and Ishmael, and the holy spring—by including several sculptural features, including a fountain, and he anchored the composition in a radial circular pattern, similar to Mecca's. Despite of lack of documentary evidence it is generally known that almost all the royal objects in the Kingdom of Saudi Arabia were built by bin Laden Construction Group, then most likely they also could have carried out the Yamasaki's projects. According to several testimonies the construction company of Mohammed bin Laden even took part in the construction of the WTC project in New York. Memorial to the United flight 93, which according to the official version fell in Shanksville Pennsylvania on September 11 of 2001 resembles the Islamic compass Quibla, which helps muslims to find direction to Mecca for prayers. The 9/11 Memorial in New York reminds us of the sacred stone of Kaaba in Mecca, which is not surprising, because such was the desire of Yamasaki himself. The metal sculpture "Sphere" of the German sculptor Fritz Koenig is now located in Battery Park, New York. Earlier the sculpture was located on the Austin Joseph Tobin Square, next to the towers of the World Trade Center in Manhattan. After the attacks of September 11, 2001, it was removed from the wreckage and sent for temporary storage to a warehouse near the John F. Kennedy International Airport. The sphere was placed on a ring in the center of the fountain and, along with the decorative elements designed by the architect Minoru Yamasaki. It was supposed to imitate the Great Mosque of Mecca, Masjid al-Haram, in which the sculpture stood in place of the sacred stone of the Kaaba.

The abovementioned Memorial to United flight 93 was a complex opened at the site of the crash of flight 93 of United Airlines, stolen during the attacks of 911. The memorial, dedicated to 40 passengers of Flight 93, which prevented according to the official version the terrorists who captured the plane from reaching their destination. It located 3.2 km north of Shanksville and 97 km southeast of Pittsburgh. The temporary monument was opened shortly after the disaster, and the permanent monument was completed in 2011, by the 10th anniversary of the terrorist attacks. Architects who were commissioned this project - Paul and Milena Murdoch.

Qiblah - in Islam, the direction from the direction of the sacred Kaaba in Mecca in Arabia, established from all points of the globe, observed by all Muslims during five daily prayers and the dispatch of a series of rituals. Qibla is of great importance in the construction of mosques and other Islamic religious buildings, as well as serves as a symbol of spiritual unity. But this "coincidental' resemblance was not enough for the authors of the project. They went even further with "Tower of voices" in a form of minaret with a crescent directed at the sky, which is especially noticeable when you stand at its base. After the scandal, cosmetic changes were made to the memorial, designed to cover the Islamic theme with a fig leaf but in fact, nothing was changed. In a conversation with the correspondent of the portal of Yahoo on 2.09.11 architect Paul Murdoch justified the Islamic design of the memorial quite unconvincingly:

I read that the original design was a crescent, but that was changed after some criticism about the use of that symbol in the design. [Critics of the design perceived the shape to mimic an Islamic symbol.] Were you surprised by the controversy?

"It was a surprise. The intention was to create a monumental gesture of embracing that place. If you think of a tragic event, or something that happens to a friend of yours, and you see them, one of the things you do, is embrace. We took that very personal idea and did it at a scale that is in keeping with the land -- in a heroic scale commensurate with a national memorial commemorating an event.

We called that element "crescent of embrace," giving a whole new meaning to the form. Some folks didn't take it that way. They read other symbolism that was, of course, not at all what we had in mind. To eliminate any kind of conflict, we ended up adding more trees to that area so it's more fully a circle.

Have you noticed any change in the attitudes and perception of the memorial project? What, specifically, is different from back then and now?

I think the flare-up was pretty peripheral. The thrust has been with a lot of support to get this thing in the ground and open. That's where everybody has been putting their efforts. That's where the support has been. We're enjoying the fruits of that focus, not some peripheral nonsense. I think it's important to recognize that there are a lot of challenges to do something like this. So that we're opening this important phase 10 years after the event is actually an achievement. It seems like a long time coming, but I think it's a big first step."

On the right is the original design, left after the corrections when the authors tried to plant new trees and close the crescent.

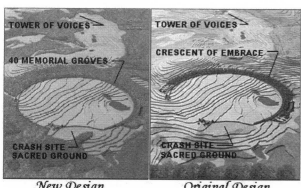

New Design
"40 Memorial Groves"

Original Design
"Crescent of Embrace"

Tower of voices

The Islamic crescent design of the monument is not a coincidence because its central axis points exactly to Mecca.

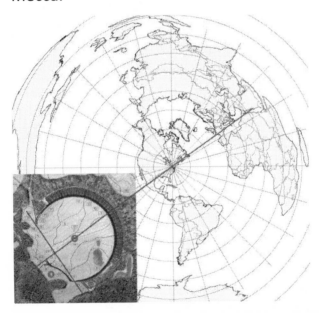

Let's return to Francis Bacon and the Bible of King James. Beside of the fact that psalm 46 is located in the original version or facsimile versions on page 666 it also placed in chapter 666 counting from the end.

By chance or not but in the same psalm 46th in Bible of King James 46th word from the beginning of the stanza and

46th from the end of it, we find the name "Shakespeare". The rumor of Francis Bacon being the real author of Shakespeare's works had been circulating even during his lifetime, but I have cryptographic evidence that he, possibly along with a team of best literary talents of England, was a real "Shakespeare".

If we seriously consider the hypothesis that the genuine author of Shakespeare's plays was the titan of thought, the occultist and the polymath, Sir Francis Bacon, who was the editor of the King James Bible, if not the author of entire KJV project, then such "coincidences" are not accidental. If you look in the encyclopedia, some of them indicate the birthday of Shakespeare on April 23, others April 26. To be precise, Shakespeare's birth date, whoever he was, is unknown, but the date of baptism is known precisely-April 26. A typical practice of those times in England was to baptize on the 3rd day after birth.

"There are many considerations regarding the participation of Shakespeare in translating the poetic part (psalms and Solomon's Song) of the King James Bible. The proof is given by cryptographic evidence. It is alleged that Shakespeare was born on April 23, 1564 and died April 23, 1616th. The sum of 23 + 23 gives 46. The Bible of King James was published in 1611, when Shakespeare was 46 years old. The name "William Shakespeare" can be read as an anagram of "Here I was, like a psalm".

" The Mystery of King James " by Philip Depois

However, a precise calculation of the location in the Bible of the same Psalm 46 is a much more convincing proof than the above. There are many other indicators of the real authorship of Shakespeare's works.

The last verse of Psalm 46 is 1776th according to the account from the end of the Psalms. By a strange "coincidence," the Freedom Tower (World Trade Center of the One World) has a height of 1,776 feet, which is also the year of the founding of the famous Order of the Bavarian Illuminati by Adam Weishaupt in Ingolstadt. The King James Bible consists of 66 books (another coincidence).

I do not know if this is a coincidence or another secret code in the King James Bible of the year, but in Chapter 3 of Genesis, where the snake (tempting devil) persuades Eva to try the forbidden fruit from the Tree of Knowledge, he does it exactly in 46 words. "Yea, hath God said, Ye shall not eat of every tree of the garden? -14

Ye shall not surely die. -5

For God, doth know that in the day ye eat thereof, then your eyes shall be opened, and ye shall be as gods, knowing good and evil. "-27 Words 14 + 5 + 27 = 46

Above I have repeatedly mentioned the name Rockefeller in connection with the "project 911". To any American schoolchild, long before September 11, 2001 it was known that 911 is the emergency number. The number was introduced in 1968 "at the suggestion of AT & T." In 1967, the President's Commission on Law Enforcement and Administration of Justice recommended the creation of a single number that could be used nationwide for reporting emergencies. The Federal Communications Commission then met with AT&T in November 1967 in order to choose the number.

In 1968, the number was agreed upon. AT&T chose the number 9-1-1, which was simple, easy to remember, dialed easily, and worked well with the phone systems in place at the time. At the time, this announcement only affected the Bell System telephone companies; independent phone companies were not included in the emergency telephone plan. However, Bob Gallagher of the Alabama Telephone Company decided he wanted to implement it ahead of AT&T, and the company chose Haleyville, Alabama, as the location." This is what states official version of creation of emergency number 911. If you recall those times or even the films of those years , then you will realize that the absolute majority of phones had a dial-disc and the first button phones began to appear only in the early 70's. Imagine a dial-drive, where 9 and 1 are on opposite sides of the disk, so you'd have to put your finger in two different dial slots. This number cannot be called fast and convenient, since any other combination of 3 identical numbers where one would not have to rearrange a finger on the dial would be much more efficient. From this is absolutely clear that the real goals differed from those declared by AT & T. In the financial literature of the 1960s, it was still possible to find references to the fact that AT & T is controlled by the Rockefeller interests, now nothing of the kind can be found. You can track the institutional shareholders of the company, but you will not see the list of private investors, and besides you won't know who is hiding behind the two largest shareholders - Vanguard Group and Blackrock. However, what Rockefeller structure is hiding behind which of the investment funds for our investigation is not important at all. We follow the cryptographic "fingerprints" and they are available in abundance.

Is there a direct link with the emergency number 911 and the September 11 date? Yes, there is and President Reagan had indicated that even twice to us.

President Ronald Reagan signed on September 9, 1983, the proclamation of the day **11 .9**. 83 as "National Day of Mourning" for the passengers of South Korean Boeing, flight KAL 007 which had been shot down over the USSR on 1.9.83 (19 and 8 + 3 = 11 = 911).

On August 26 (88), 1987, President Reagan proclaimed September 11 "The National Day of the emergency call number 911". The US Congress made this proclamation a federal law numbered 99-448. Thus, the psychological preprogramming of the population through the compulsory association of September 11 and 911 with sorrow began long before the main event on 11.09.01.

Proclamation 5093 of September 9, 1983

National Day of Mourning
Sunday, September 11, 1983

By the President of the United States of America
A Proclamation
To the People of the United States:

September 1, 1983, will be seared in the minds of civilized people everywhere as the night of the Korean Air Lines Massacre. Two hundred sixty-nine innocent men, women and children, from 13 different countries, who were flying aboard KAL flight 007, were stalked, then shot out of the air and sent crashing to their deaths by a missile aimed and fired by the Soviet Union.

Good and decent people everywhere are filled with revulsion by this despicable deed, and by the refusal of the guilty to tell the truth. This was a crime against humanity that must never be forgotten, here or throughout the world.

We open our hearts in prayer to the victims and their families. We earnestly beseech Almighty God to minister to them in their trial of grief, sorrow, and pain.

In their memory, we ask all people who cherish individual rights, and who believe each human life is sacred, to come together in a shared spirit of wisdom, unity, courage, and love, so the world can prevent such an inhuman act from ever happening again.

NOW, THEREFORE, I, RONALD REAGAN, President of the United States of America, in tribute to the memory of the slain passengers of Korean Air Lines flight 007, and as an expression of public sorrow, do hereby appoint Sunday, September 11, 1983, to be a National Day of Mourning throughout the United States. I recommend that the people assemble on that day in

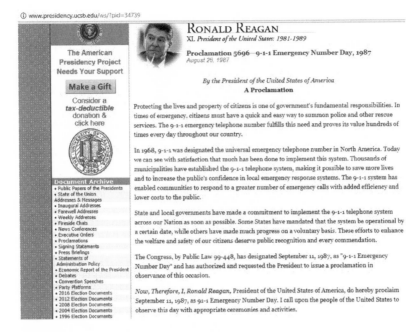

RONALD REAGAN
XL *President of the United States: 1981-1989*

Proclamation 5696—9-1-1 Emergency Number Day, 1987
August 26, 1987

The American
Presidency Project
Needs Your Support

Make a Gift

Consider a
tax-deductible
donation &
click here

By the President of the United States of America
A Proclamation

Protecting the lives and property of citizens is one of government's fundamental responsibilities. In times of emergency, citizens must have a quick and easy way to summon police and other rescue services. The 9-1-1 emergency telephone number fulfills this need and proves its value hundreds of times every day throughout our country.

In 1968, 9-1-1 was designated the universal emergency telephone number in North America. Today we can see with satisfaction that much has been done to implement this system. Thousands of municipalities have established the 9-1-1 telephone system, making it possible to save more lives and to increase the public's confidence in local emergency response systems. The 9-1-1 system has enabled communities to respond to a greater number of emergency calls with added efficiency and lower costs to the public.

State and local governments have made a commitment to implement the 9-1-1 telephone system across our Nation as soon as possible. Some States have mandated that the system be operational by a certain date, while others have made much progress on a voluntary basis. These efforts to enhance the welfare and safety of our citizens deserve public recognition and every commendation.

The Congress, by Public Law 99-448, has designated September 11, 1987, as "9-1-1 Emergency Number Day" and has authorized and requested the President to issue a proclamation in observance of this occasion.

Now, Therefore, I, Ronald Reagan, President of the United States of America, do hereby proclaim September 11, 1987, as 91-1 Emergency Number Day. I call upon the people of the United States to observe this day with appropriate ceremonies and activities.

Document Archive
• Public Papers of the Presidents
• State of the Union
Addresses & Messages
• Inaugural Addresses
• Farewell Addresses
• Weekly Addresses
• Fireside Chats
• News Conferences
• Executive Orders
• Proclamations
• Signing Statements
• Press Briefings
• Statements of
Administration Policy
• Economic Report of the President
• Debates
• Convention Speeches
• Party Platforms
• 2016 Election Documents
• 2012 Election Documents
• 2008 Election Documents
• 2004 Election Documents
• 1996 Election Documents

Chapter VIII. Der Neunte Elfte

The surrender of Germany in World War I has been marked by the signing of the Compiègne Armistice on November 11 (911) 1918, at 6 am (9), after which all military operations were seized at 11 o'clock. Thus, the end of the war took place under the shadow of the symbolic code 911 manifested several times: November (the 9th month of the Roman calendar, from the Latin novem), on the 11th day of the month-911, at 6 o'clock in the morning the treaty was signed, at 11 o'clock the guns were silenced (6 = 9) 911. The end of the war ended with a salute of 101 guns. (11,droping the zero)

"At 11 o'clock the first shots of the artillery salute of the nations were heard with 101 volleys, which ushered the end of the First World War."

Here is the long list of the "coincidences" involving 11s associated with events of September 11

(9+1+1) =11

"New York City"-11 letters

"The Pentagon" – 11 letters

New York=111 in simple gematria

New York=666 in Sumerian gematria

New York is the 11th state

Flight 11 had 11 crew members and 81 passengers (8+1)=9. 11+81=92… (9+2)=11

The second tower collapsed in 9 seconds

The first tower collapsed in 11 seconds

The first plane to hit the towers was Flight 11

Flight 11 had 92 on board (9+2)= 11

Towers were 110 stories tall. In numerology zeros don't count because they have no value so you have another 11.

September 11th is the 254th day of the year. 254: (2+5+4)=11

September 11th leaves 111 days remaining in the year

The Hollywood movie United 93 is about 911 and runs exactly 111 minutes in length

David Rockefeller proposed the towers to his brother Nelson Rockefeller

Rockefeller=110 in simple gematria…. 11 in numerology

Rockefeller=56 in English reduction gematria (5+6)=11

The World Trade Center was built between 1966 to 1977 which is a span of 11 years.

The south tower burnt for 56 minutes. (5+6=)11

The north tower collapsed at 10:28 (1+2+8)=11

21,800 windows per tower (2+1+8+0+0)= 11

Flight 77 (11×7) had 65on board(6+5) = 11

March 11th or 3/11, is when the Tribute in Lights started in remembrance for 911. 3/11 can also be looked at as three 11s. 11 11 11 or (3×11)=33

The twin towers themselves resembled a huge 11 looking over NYC landscape

The first plane to hit the Twin Towers was flight AA: A=1 ...AA=11

Building 7 fell later that day and was 47 floors tall. (4+7)=11

There are 3,119 days between the 93' bombings and the 911 attacks. 119 is 911 backwards.

The attacks were blamed on Osama bin Laden who equals 110 (15+19+1+13+1+2+9+14+12+1+4+5+14=110)

The first project 9/11 on a national scale was carried out in Germany. There the date symbolizing 911 is November 9 (9th day of the 11th month). This date was dubbed "Fateful day". It was on November 9 that Philippe Scheidemann proclaims the German Republic in 1918. On November 9, 1923, Hitler and his co-conspirators arranged a coup attempt, known to us under the name "Beer Putsch." From this day on it became the most sacred of holidays for the NSDAP (Nazi party) and National Socialist State after 1933. Der Neunte Elfte-literally "Ninth of Eleven" is all the same 911. Every year on this date, starting from 1933, the solemn march of the top NSDAP leadership in memory of the "16 martyrs" of the failed coup took place. In Munich monumental "Temple of Honor" has been erected where 16 martyrs were buried. In this case 16 martyrs of Hittler's failed coup and 19 Arab terrorists of September 11 of 2001 might not be coincidental 16=19 (remember interchangeable 9 and 6)

November 9, 1925 is considered the official birthday of the SS, when its troops received the official name - "SS of the National Socialist German Workers' Party" (German Die SS der NSDAP). November 9, 1938 is also a bloody Jewish pogrom throughout Germany, which became known as the "Crystal Night".

November 9, 1989 is the day of the fall of the infamous Berlin Wall, which was debated in the Bundestag (German Parliament) to proclaim it a national holiday. However, unpleasant and probably too strong associations with 11.9.01 forced legislators to declare a holiday of German unity on October 3.

Hitler 9/11/1938 on the march of memory in honor of the Beer Putsch

Temple of Honor in Munich (now demolished)

In the light of interesting coincidences of Hitler, Rockefeller's and the very date of 911 in words (Nine One One) in two gematric systems, I have a strong suspicion that Der Neunte Elfte is something more than just a "Fateful day" in the history of the country.

Adolf Hitler in English Gematria Equals: **660** ($\frac{a\ d\ o\ l\ f\ \_h\ i\ t\ l\ e\ r}{6\ 24\ 90\ 72\ 36\ ^0\ 48\ 54\ 120\ 72\ 30\ 108}$)

Adolf Hitler in Simple Gematria Equals: **110** ($\frac{a\ d\ o\ l\ f\ \_h\ i\ t\ l\ e\ r}{1\ 4\ 15\ 12\ 6\ ^0\ 8\ 9\ 20\ 12\ 5\ 18}$)

Rockefeller in English Gematria Equals: **660** ($\frac{r\ o\ c\ k\ e\ f\ e\ l\ l\ e\ r}{108\ 90\ 18\ 66\ 30\ 36\ 30\ 72\ 72\ 30\ 108}$)

Rockefeller in Simple Gematria Equals: **110** ($\frac{r\ o\ c\ k\ e\ f\ e\ l\ l\ e\ r}{18\ 15\ 3\ 11\ 5\ 6\ 5\ 12\ 12\ 5\ 18}$)

Nine One One in English Gematria Equals: **660** ($\frac{n\ i\ n\ e\ \_o\ n\ e\ \_o\ n\ e}{84\ 54\ 84\ 30\ ^0\ 90\ 84\ 30\ ^0\ 90\ 84\ 30}$)

Nine One One in Simple Gematria Equals: **110** ($\frac{n\ i\ n\ e\ \_o\ n\ e\ \_o\ n\ e}{14\ 9\ 14\ 5\ ^0\ 15\ 14\ 5\ ^0\ 15\ 14\ 5}$)

At the same time, we must remember that Hitler was not an accidental figure, not an ordinary village fool who accidentally, but democratically came to power. There is a mass of evidence about the financing of Hitler's marginal party by the largest banks from Wall Street. Moreover, the Bush clan, in particular Prescott Bush, already mentioned earlier, played not the last role in this story. In the summer of 1942, the New York Times ran the headline on the front page: "Hitler's angels have $ 3 million in a US bank." It was about the New York investment bank Union Banking Corporation (UBC), which was headed by Prescott Bush, a grandfather and father of two former US presidents. Bush then got off with a slap on his wrists and in the early 50s even managed to return the confiscated money, but his patrons and accomplices from Standard Oil, Brown Brothers Harriman did not suffer any losses at all from US government actions. In 1933, before Hitler was appointed Chancellor of Germany a curious brochure was published in Holland in a very small number, which was called in translation from the Dutch language "Hitler's secret backers. 3 talks with Hitler." The brochure was signed by a certain Sydney Warburg, a fictitious character who, however, did not tell a completely fictitious story about how the leading bankers from Wall Street participated in the financing of the desperate NSDAP between 1928-1933. The book was immediately withdrawn from circulation, either by Hitler's agents or by other of the interested parties. Judging by the description of the manners of Hitler's speech in the little book, the man did indeed meet repeatedly with Adolf Hitler. This brochure has been mentioned in the memoirs of Vice-Chancellor von Papen in the post-war period, which he called a fake. As is it known today, one of the originals of this pamphlet was in the hands of later deposed by Austria's Anschluss chancellor Kurt Schuschnigg. Perhaps this book played an important role in further destiny of Schuschnigg after the Anschluss with Reich. Let me summarize that the mere fact of massive financial support of one of the marginal German party, with its not quite adequate leader, probably was in line with both political, financial, and occult interests from both centers of financial power-New York and London. Hitler's NSDAP was not likely to win 1933 elections and party had serious financial problems. Somebody needed to see the gain in Hitler's coming to power and make a massive investment even though that on surface that might mean doing harm to US and other European countries interests.

Chapter IX Personal Hitler's magician

The interest in occult by Adolf Hitler himself and the top leaders of the Third Reich is well documented, although not widely publicized for the masses. The Austrian medium, the telepath, the astrologer and the occultist Hermann Steinschneider, better known by his pseudonym Erik Jan Hanussen, made a dazzling career in Germany, advising top officials of the Nazi Party on various issues. Native of Vienna he started his career in Austria by solving crimes for local police. However, his "exploits" aimed at combating crime earned him a hostile attitude on the part of the Vienna Police Directory, which for some reason suspected him of committing the very crimes, which he then solved, or in possession of insider information. But

Hanussen found at least one patron among the police officials. Dr. Leopold Toma was a psychoanalyst, paranormal researcher and head of the psychological and pedagogical department of the Vienna police. In 1921 he created his own institute of "Criminal telepathic science". In a few years his ways and Hanussen's will cross again. Hanussen resonant telepathic performances at La Scala and other theaters were attended by such celebrities as Marlene Dietrich, Sigmund Freud, Peter Lorre, Fritz Lang and Hermann Goering. Hanussen bought expensive cars, a yacht and a plane, as well as a small publishing empire of books, magazines and newspapers that relentlessly promoted his psychic abilities and his astrological predictions. Hanussen, despite his Jewish background, was very popular among high-ranking Nazi party officials.

In his popular "Colored Weekly of Hanussen" he published astrological stock exchange forecasts and even correctly predicted the fire of the Reichstag in 1933. How and from whom Hanussen received this information is still unknown. In his editions Hanussen predicted the victory of the National Socialism in Germany. He advised Adolf Hitler himself, and his exact pro-Nazi predictions earned Hanussen the nicknames "The Prophet of the Third Reich", "Nazi Rasputin", "Hitler's Nostradamus" and others.

He provided private loans to "special friends", among whom were prominent Nazis such as Wolf Heinrich, Graf von Helldorf, head of the SA organization in Berlin, a gambler and a famous connoisseur of "black magic."

Whatever his occult abilities were, Hanussen was a clever, unprincipled and corrupt character, who had ability to rubb into the confidence to influential people in Germany. He clearly had a talent for accessing sensitive information. His influence as an informant only increased when he gained personal access to Hitler. Apparently, Hanussen employed skills that he had earned in the Viennese magazine Der Blitz, which made its main money by blackmailing the objects of its journalistic investigations, withholding scandalous materials from the publication. His wealth was multiplied by means of blackmail (as in the days of Der Blitz). Called by Mel Gordon "Master of Sex Ludy", Hanussen conducted and secretly filmed private sessions, which were frequented by politicians, aristocrats, movie stars and industrialists. There were perverted orgies, where some guests found themselves in a compromised position and were willing to pay for silence. Author Mel Gordon had gathered a lot of such materials on Hanussen's life in Germany in his book "Erik Jan Hanussen: Hitler's Jewish Clairvoyant"

On the morning of April 7, 1933 South of Berlin, the workers came across a gruesome discovery. Near the road that connected the German capital with the city of Barut, a riddled body of a man dressed in evening clothes was found. Death came from two shots in the head. The corpse was covered with larvae, and the animals gnawed at the face, which made it almost unrecognizable. The investigator of Berlin's criminal police Hermann Albrecht quickly determined that the deceased was Eric Jan Hanussen, a famous Berlin clairvoyant and astrologer who had disappeared two weeks ago. Apparently, Albrecht was aware beforehand that the real murderers were people from the SA who, apparently on Hitler's personal order, got rid of a man who knew too much. The official version of Albrecht, however, is that the murder was committed by "Berlin gangsters."

Interestingly, another occultist, who also settled in Berlin between 1930-32, was infamous Alistair Crowley. Crowley had lengthy ties with British intelligence, and part of his goal of arriving in Germany was to watch some interesting people. Given Hanusen's notoriety and his fame in hypnotism, "Great Beast 666" (Crowley's nickname) could not have ignored him. Ironically, Crowley's diaries do not contain a single mention of Hanussen or anything related to him.

Nevertheless, there was indirect link between two occultists. By 1930 the above-mentioned Dr. Leopold Toma appeared again in the life of Hanusen and became one of his closest associates. Toma has been well acquainted with another Austrian psychoanalyst, Alfred Adler, a man whom Crowley claimed to have known personally and worked with him in Berlin. Moreover, Toma made friends with Dr. Alexander Cannon, another psychiatrist, a paranormal researcher and a friend of Crowley, whose roads intersected with Hanussen. Cannon, sometimes called the Yorkshire Yogi, or the "leader of black magic in England," would later be accused of being a supporter of the Nazis and even of being a German spy. Finally, Hanussen was a confidant of Hans Heinz Evers, a German writer and occultist, who at that time was a passionate adherent of National Socialism's ideology, who had access to Hitler. In addition, Evers was an old friend of Crowley. Thus, Crowley had several channels through which he could obtain information about Hanussen and what he knew.

Crowley-Hanussen's relationship could be base of Rene Gennon's later claim that "The Beast 666" penetrated Hitler's inner circle and even became a "secret adviser" to the Nazi leader. There is no documentary evidence that Crowley managed to get any close to the future Fuhrer, which undoubtedly, Hanussen did succeed.

It is also likely that Toma worked for Austrian intelligence. The Vienna Police Directory, with which he remained connected, was involved in intelligence and counterintelligence activities. Finding out what was on the mind of their compatriot Adolf Hitler would be the primary task of the Directory. Hanussen, in this respect, may have been a very valuable source of information.

In 1933, Pierre Mariel, a writer associated with French intelligence, wrote a curious book, "The Seven Heads of the Green Dragon"under the pseudonym Teddy Legrand. He claimed to have discovered the machinations of an international conspiracy that was behind Hitler's rise to power. Hanussen appears in the book thinly disguised funder the character of the agent "Man with green gloves." Years later, in a book on Nazi occultism, Mariel claimed that "Hanussen was a British spy," based on the confession of former British agent John Goldsmith. If there were no secret agencies that had exploited Hanussen, then certainly, they should have been.

Erik Jan Hanussen holds a séance of spiritism

Aleister Crowley

Chapter X The occult origins of the National Socialism

The occult beliefs of Nazi Germany generally deserve a separate book. All the available materials on this topic that I have accumulated is enough for at least 500 pages text. A well-known and indisputable fact is the commitment of the leaders of the Third Reich to various mystical practices of the East, especially Tibetan. Moreover, with the Tibetan monks, the Nazis began a relationship back in the mid of 1920s. It remains unclear though why Buddhist monks experienced such a sympathy toward National Socialism. Nonetheless several historical and research expeditions were undertaken by the Germans in Tibet in the late 1930s were crowned with complete success. Ernst Schaefer made at least 3 successful expeditions to Tibet, using the personal patronage of Reichsfuhrer Heinrich Himmler. There was an hour and a half documentary of Schaefer's expedition under the name "Mysterious Tibet", which was intended only for private viewing among SS members. Himmler and Hitler were even more motivated to search for the enigmatic Shambhala than Dzerzhinsky's secret police in Russia. Significant funds were allocated to finance expeditions. They exported to Germany tens and hundreds of parchments in Sanskrit and ancient Chinese. Werner von Braun, the creator of the first rockets and founder of NASA's Apollo program, once said: "We learned a lot from these papers." The hero of Brad Pitt in the film "7 Years in Tibet" by Jean Jacques Annaud, actually went to Tibet on Himmler's secret assignment. After the release of the movie Nazi past of Brad Pitt's hero has been discovered. Heinrich Harrer, who was portrayed by Pitt denied his membership in the SS until his death, calling it only "formal" (which was never the case with a special selection of its members), and completely denied that he went to Tibet on Himmler's personal assignment. The Dalai Lama, who was practically brought up by Harrer, also tried to obscure his Nazi sympathy and his close relationship with Harrer, whom he supported until the death of the mountain climber. During the siege of Berlin by the Red Army in 1945, the officers were surprised to find the corpses of Asians, who were Tibetans dressed in the uniform of the Wehrmacht.

For study and search of Ubermensch(Super human), Shambhala and other mythical purposes in 1935 has been established the organization Annenerbe (Legacy of the Ancestors) . The roots of Anenerbe should be sought both in the activities of the esoteric society "Thul", and in the hypotheses and ideas of a number of individuals, such as the scientist Hermann Wirth and the occultist Friedrich Hilscher (the tutor of the future secretary-general of "Anenerbe" Wolframm Sievers). Hilscher spoke with the Swedish researcher Sven Gedin, a former orientalist who spent many years in Tibet, as well as with Professor Karl Haushofer (a professor at the University of Munich, whose assistant was young Rudolf Hess). Hess introduced Haushofer to Hitler, who was fascinated by the idea of conquest of the "living space"(Lebensraum), various occult-mystical constructions and hypotheses. In 1937, Himmler invited Schaeffer to join the society Ahnenerbe to have a greater influence on him. He also promised him unlimited financial opportunities. Ahnenerbe spent a lot of money to achieve the goals that Elena Blavatsky had already formulated in her "Secret Doctrine". Among the mystic theorists who stood at the origins of the ideology of Nazism were Guido von List and George Lanz von Liebenfels, they were all inspired by the works of the same Elena Petrovna Blavatsky and the ideas of the Theosophical Society. As I wrote above, Hitler greatly appreciated Blavatsky's book "The Secret Doctrine" and tried to implement its postulates in practice.

Sturmbannfuhrer Ernst Schaeffer during one of the Tibetan expeditions

Heinrich Harrer left from Adolf Hitler. Below Harrer and Dalai Lama

Der schönste Lohn

Harrer (links neben Hitler): „Kinder was habt ihr geleistet!"

An interesting question is if Adolf Hitler was personally a member of one of the influential secret societies? On this issue, there is no clarity, although Hitler's official statements have always had been anti-Masonic. The Masonic lodges on the territory of the Reich have been officially suppressed. According to the official data of the Masonic historians of Germany, not only all the lodges ceased to exist, but many of their members also ended up in prisons and concentration camps. All this seems to be an indisputable historical fact. But with a detailed examination of the chronicles of individual lodges, it turns out that everything happened not at once. In 1935, the Masonic lodges of Germany continue, as if nothing happened, to correspond with each other through normal mail about the demand of the Nazi party for the withdrawal of its members from Masonic lodges, in connection with the demand for the dissolution of Masonic organizations. In 1934 the Grand Lodge of Germany renamed itself the "German-Christian Order". The activity of Masonic lodges does not cease in the following years. In 1937 the Grand Lodge of Germany, already renamed, informs its members about the foundation in the city of Neidenburg of the association of masons of higher degrees "Zur Velhat". By 1935 the journal of attendance of the members of the chapter "indesolubilis" in Berlin (No. 8917) is still can be found in the archives. The Chapter is the supreme governing body of the United Masonic Lodges. At the same time the activities were undertaken to transform the Order. This topic is devoted in the circulars of the Grand Lodge "Royal York" in Berlin (No. 7502)

In 1934 a new lodge was created in Koenigsberg, but in Tilsit the Gestapo confiscated the property of the lodge "Guene" in the same year. It seems this is the beginning of the end, but the documents otherwise. The Lodge of "Andrew Strenua" in the same Tilsit prospers until 1939, and the "Irene" Lodge was quietly liquidated only in early 1940s. The Grand Lodge of Germany corresponds with the "Zur Edle Aussicht" in Freiburg on the accession of its members to the Nazi Party. In Breslau, the case of the liquidation of the Montana Lodge stretched from 1933 to 1938. From all that is obvious that situation with Masonic lodges in Nazi Germany was not that dire as it was portrayed by Masonic historians for the general public in later times. The documents prove that there were members of the NSDAP who were still members of Masonic lodges contrary to the official version of complete ban on Freemasonry during Third Reich.

Variety of photographs and artistic portraits of both Adolf Hitler and other significant figures in the hierarchy of the Third Reich show that there was something that remained outside the official chronicles. There is no document or evidence that speaks in favor of the version that Hitler ever joined any of the Masonic lodges in Austria or Germany. But photographs cannot lie, especially since their authenticity has never been disputed by any expert.

Photos of Masonic handshakes of Hitler, as they were illustrated in the book of Captain Morgan in 1827

On the compilation below you see an assortment of secret signs that are used in Freemasonry, and one sign in particular, the origin of which is still not clear. On several photographs, and on the portrait by the painter Knirre,

Hitler is depicted with a gesture of the hand reminding the outlines of the letters W or M. It is known that many Masons use this sign, but its significance is unknown. The sign is seen on hundreds of portraits of famous artists, beginning from the first half of the XVI century. In addition, that on one of the photos Hitler points to this sign with the index finger of the other hand. There is a similar gesture on the photographs of Elvis Presley and actor James Dean in exactly the same pose. In the compilation of this strange hand gestures below you'll find the poster of the movie "M" from 1931 by the famous Austrian director Fritz Lang with the same hand gesture. Fritz Land has been mentioned above in connection with the story of Hitler's psychic Hanussen. Lang is also the author of the film "Metropolis" with a massive occult undercurrent, which he released in Germany in 1927. On the poster of "M" you see a palm of the hand, which displays same gesture similar to that of on Hitler's portrait. Lang also was the director of the science fiction film "Woman on the Moon", which inspired Werner von Braun in his research in rocket technology. On his V1 and V2 rockets, which bombed London, he portrayed a main heroine of the film. In his youth von Braun was lucky enough to work as a technician on the set of Lang's "Women on the Moon". Later Lang also succeeded in Hollywood. The other secret gestures are visible on the portraits of Walter Schellenberg and General Karl Wolff are known and well-studied. The gesture of the fist pressed to the chest is called "lion's paw" in Freemasonry, and the hand at the chest hidden in the jacket- is the "secret hand" or "the master of the second veil". The "lion's paw" gesture is often masked by the grabbing of the lapel of the jacket or an "arbitrary" posture, supported by the back of the chair. The history of membership in the Masonic lodges of historical figures is usually thoroughly documented in their biographies, in addition to eloquent photographs or artistic portraits. So, it is always possible to match the portraits displaying secret gestures with their involvement in Freemasonry. In some cases, there is nothing in their biographies about membership in Masonic or other secret lodges, but you could rely on their portraits, which is even more genuine document than official biography. There are several portraits of Werner von Braun with the "lion's paw" gesture. These gestures indicate a low degree of Masonic initiation, but they date back to the time when, according to official history, the members of the NSDAP, especially on the higher positions, were not allowed to be members of the Masonic lodges. The other two high ranking Nazi officials displaying Masonic gestures in the compilation below are Walter Schellenberg and General Karl Wolf. Schellenberg rose through the ranks of the SS, becoming one of the highest-ranking men in the Sicherheitsdienst (SD) and eventually assumed the position as head of foreign intelligence for Nazi Germany following the abolition of the Abwehr in 1944. After the war, Schellenberg was arrested by British military police and eventually stood trial in Nuremberg. On 4 November 1949, he was sentenced to six years in prison for his role in the murder of Soviet POWs who were employed as agents in Operation Zeppelin.During the postwar Nuremberg Trials, Schellenberg testified about the SS organisation and the Nazi leaders in its fold. During the Ministries Trial, he wrote his memoirs, The Labyrinth. Historian Robert Gerwarth describes certain content of Schellenberg's memoirs as "questionable". He was released from prison after two years on the grounds of ill-health, due to a worsening liver condition, and moved to Switzerland, before settling in Verbania Pallanza, Italy. He died in Turin, Italy in 1952

Karl Wolff was a high-ranking member of the Nazi SS who held the rank of SS-Obergruppenführer in the Waffen-SS. He became Chief of Personal Staff Reichsführer-SS (Heinrich Himmler) and SS Liaison Officer to Hitler until his replacement in 1943. He ended World War II as the Supreme Commander of all SS forces in Italy. Wolff evaded prosecution at the Nuremberg Trials, apparently as a result of his participation in Operation Sunrise. In 1964, Wolff was convicted of war crimes in West Germany; he was released in 1969. There is nothing in biographies of these two men which could shed the light on their membership in secret societies, but pictures don't lie.

John Bulwer, a follower of Sir Francis Bacon, in his treatise "The Chronology of the Natural Language of Hands", published in the middle of the sixteenth century, does not explain the significance of the gesture, which he himself demonstrates in the portrait of a contemporary.

Masonic post card from 1908 with the man displaying M-W sign

The website of Grand Lodge of British Columbia telling the story confirming authenticity of these post card series

On this picture, Wolf Heinrich Count von Helldorf (the same patron of the psychic Hanussen) in the center shows a sign of the "lion's paw". On the right is Joseph Goebbels. Wolf-Heinrich Countvon Helldorf (November 14, 1896,

Merseburg - August 15, 1944, Berlin) - politician and
statesman, member of the NSDAP, Obergruppenfuhrer SA
(1933), SS Obergruppenfiihrer and police general (1938),
Reichstag deputy, Chief of police Podsdam and Berlin.
Executed for participating in a conspiracy against Hitler.

Fig 2: Walther Schellenberg (*left*); Wernher von Braun (*right*)

Werner von Braun right and Walter Schellenberg with
"lion's paw" hand sign

Hand sign "hidden hand"(master of the second veil).
Architect Bartholdi, writers Edgar Alan Poe, Fyodor
Dostoyevsky, scientist Charles Darwin

Chapter XI Esoteric origin of Code 88

There is a basic concept in astronomy called "analemma"
which is for some strange reason is not taught in schools.

In astronomy, an analemma from Greek ἀνάλημμα
"support") is a diagram showing the variation of the
position of the Sun in the sky over the course of a year, as
viewed at a fixed time of day and from a fixed location on

the Earth. The north–south component of the analemma is due to change of the Sun's declination caused by the tilt of the Earth's axis, and the east–west component is due to nonuniform rate of change of the Sun's right ascension, governed by combined effects of axial tilt and Earth's orbital eccentricity. The diagram has the form of a slender figure eight and can often be found on globes of the Earth. In order to understand what analemma has to do with Freemasonry one has to understand the esoterical meaning of Masonic tracing board. Tracing boards are painted or printed illustrations depicting the various emblems and symbols of Freemasonry. They can be used as teaching aids during the lectures that follow each of the Masonic Degrees, when an experienced member explains the various concepts of Freemasonry to new members. They can also be used by experienced members as self-reminders of the concepts they learned as they went through their initiations. The most frequent protagonists of the Masonic tracing board are the pillars of Boaz and Jachin, above which is usually depicted the Moon and the Sun. From the very beginning of civilization, the entrance to sacred and mysterious places was guarded by two pillars. In art or architecture, double pillars are archetypal symbols, representing important gates or portals to the unknown. In Masonry, the pillars are called Jachin and Boaz and represent one of the most recognizable symbols of the Brotherhood, adorning any Masonic lodgeS and temples.

The concept of double pillars, standing at the gates of sacred places, can be traced from the ancient civilizations of Antiquity.

The symbol of double pillars from time immemorial protected the gate to holy places and mysterious kingdoms. They mark the passage to the unknown and otherworldly. In ancient Greece, the "Pillars of Hercules" was a phrase that was applied to the capes that adjoined the entrance to the Strait of Gibraltar. The North Pillar is the Rock of Gibraltar in the British territory of Gibraltar. South on the Moroccan side. The pillars of Hercules guard the passage to the unknown.

According to the story of Plato, the lost kingdom of Atlantis was behind the pillars of Hercules, actually placing it in the realm of the Unknown. The Renaissance tradition says that on the pillars was a warning Nec plus ultra (also Non plus ultra, "nothing further"), which served as a warning to seamen and navigators not to go any further. It is symbolic that going beyond the pillars of Hercules could mean that the one who has turned away from the material world will attain a higher level of enlightenment. This is the Masonic interpretation. According to the Old Testament, brass, copper or bronze pillars of Boaz and Jachin preceded the entrance to the Temple built by King Solomon. Literally, Jachin means "He will confirm," and Boaz - "there is power in him." The description of the creation of the pillars of Boaz and Jachin is given in the biblical Third Book of Kings (Chapter 7, articles 15-21). It is reported in the Scriptures that the pillars of Boaz and Jachin were built by Hiram, the "son of one widow" and the tinsmith, the inhabitant of Tire (1 Samuel 7:14). Hence the Masonic legend of the "widow's son" and the code phrase of the call for help, of which I have already written above. It is the pillars of Boaz and Jachin with the Moon and the Sun above them, as it is depicted on the Masonic tracing boards and represents portals to the new world, which is symbolized by two analemmas, the double 8s that describes the movement of the heavenly bodies during the year. The twin towers were esoterically two pillars, Boaz and Jachin, a portal to the new world, a new world order, that is why both codes, 911 and 88 always go hand in hand in all the coded media production.

Solar and Lunar Analemmas-88 and Masonic tracing board

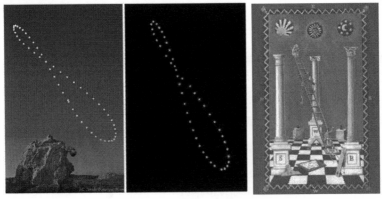

That is why it is not accidental that an inventor of the time machine from the "Back to the Future" a person named Emmett Lathrop Brown had been chosen, that reads backwards "time portal" with a minimal phonetic correction. Moreover, the surname "Brown" directly hints at the founder of NASA's Moon landing "Apollo" program, former Sturmbannfuhrer SS Werner von Braun. Doc Brown even tells Marty how his family moved to America from Germany, slightly changing the name Braun to Brown. Besides, it is no secret for serious researchers that NASA itself was in to the occult, as all the names of the space programs, as well as the biographies of its founders are indicating presence of esoteric agenda. One of the most obvious examples was Jack Parsons. To top it all off at least the first astronauts were the Masons of the highest degrees of initiation. John "Jack" Whitehead Parsons was a fanatical occultist and follower of the Telemic doctrine of Aleister Crowley. A chemical engineer and explosives specialist, he worked as a lead scientist in the experimental rocket science research group at the California Institute of Technology. Their test site at Arroyo-Seco in Pasadena has since grown to the jet engine laboratory, the center for the development and management of the American planetary exploration program. Parsons acted as co-founder of the company "Aerojet General Corporation", which intercepted the torch for production of solid-propellant rocket carriers for space shuttles after the "Challenger" disaster. Together with his first wife, Parsons joined OTO (Orden Templi Orientis) in 1941. In the Order he went headlong into occult studies. For a short time, he served as acting master of Agape Lodge, managing from a mansion in Pasadena. At that time the famous "Babalon Working" (1946) was still waiting for publication; this work changed the course of Parsons' life, completing his relationship with Alistair Crowley and O.T.O. The founder of the Church of Scientology, L. Ron Hubbard was a student of Crowley and Parsons' associate in OTO, but later their paths parted. Hubbard, too, was not a simple man, and just like Crowley himself was closely associated with the secret spy agencies. While still a naval officer, he was in the Office of Naval Intelligence. If you dig deeply into the biographies of many famous personalities who had a relationship with occult practices, from OTO to Anton LaVey's Church of Stan, most of them had connections with secret government agencies of one degree or another.

The concept of 88 is known to the Vatican, at least several hundred years. In Vatican the imaginary line from the spire of the St. Peter's Basilica to the east, through the top of the Egyptian obelisk in the center of Saint Peter's square has beating of 88 degrees. Anyone can double-check the data using Google Earth. Who exactly was author of the design is unknown to me, since even if I discard the obelisk of Caligula (Vatican obelisk), then the imaginary line of 88 degrees will pass right through the middle of Via de Concilliazione from the steeple of St. Peter's Basilica. Architects who were participating in the design of the Basilica itself are well known. From all four of them-Donato Bramante, Michelangelo, Carlo Maderno and Gian Lorenzo Bernini, it is now certain that Michelangelo was one of the artists who placed the secret codes in his works.

United States Capitol

4.5 ★★★★★ 2,403 Google reviews

Building in Washington, D.C., United States of America

| Website | Directions |

The United States Capitol, often called the Capitol Building, is the home of the United States Congress, and the seat of the legislative branch of the U.S. federal government. Wikipedia

Address: East Capitol St NE & First St SE, Washington, DC 20004, USA

Construction started: September 18, 1793

Height: 88 m

In Washington, which plan was laid out by the French architect and Freemason, Pierre Charles L'Enfant, we observe the same picture. From the spire on the Capitolium to the spire of the George Washington Monument (another obelisk) very the same 88.8 degrees. The allegory to Rome as seven hilled city and Washington where sit of power is on the Capitol hill, whose height is coincidentally, of course, 88 meters, is obvious. As I mentioned in one of the chapters above, I H S O U is the isopsephy of the Greek word Jesus-888. In the case of Washington DC, access to information is not so complicated, copies from the original blueprints of the buildings were well preserved. The entire city lay out was developed according to strict esoteric principles. The capital of the new state received an inverted unfinished pentagram, an Egyptian obelisk, an owl, a Masonic compass and a square, a hexagram (six-pointed star) amongst of any others occult symbols. The proportions of the state buildings corresponded to all occult codes.

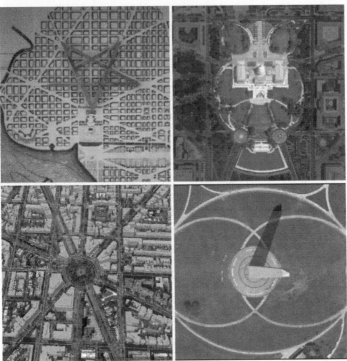

For example, the George Washington Monument in Washington DC for a long time was the world's tallest stone structure and the highest obelisk in the world. It's 555 feet high, which is **6660** inches. It was the tallest structure in the world in **1888**, until the Eiffel Tower was built a year later. The obelisk is a phallic symbol associated with the Egyptian Sun god Ra. The four sides of the Washington Monument coincide with the cardinal directions (ie, east, west, north and south). At ground level, each side of the monument has a width of 55.5 feet, which is **666** inches on each side. The height of the obelisk is 555.5 feet, which is **6,666** inches. This is the exact ratio of the golden image of King Nebuchadnezzar (which was 90 x 9 feet, ratio 10 to 1).

Lately there is a lot of media hype around of Donald Trump's person with coded mentions of number 88. On December 17, 2015, the date with the code 88 Donald Trump published a book "Winners are not losers", which makes up the English gematria 1488, the phrase "President Donald Trump" has then same number value 1488

"The 88th time Donald Trump played on the golf course as president." Do you think that this is a serious news topic beside obvious occasion to manifest the code attached to Trump's name?

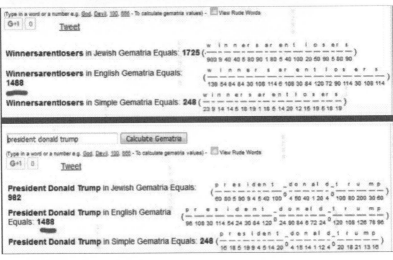

(Type in a word or a number e.g. God, Devil, 100, 666 - To calculate gematria values) - ☐ View Rude Words

G+1 0   Tweet

Winnersarentlosers in Jewish Gematria Equals: **1725**

Winnersarentlosers in English Gematria Equals: **1488**

Winnersarentlosers in Simple Gematria Equals: **248**

president donald trump   Calculate Gematria

(Type in a word or a number e.g. God, Devil, 100, 666 - To calculate gematria values) - ☐ View Rude Words

G+1 0   Tweet

President Donald Trump in Jewish Gematria Equals: **982**

President Donald Trump in English Gematria Equals: **1488**

President Donald Trump in Simple Gematria Equals: **248**

Donald Trump visited the golf course for the 88th time as President

Below portal Gawker describes a scandalous story about the PBS television report, where volunteer agitators in Trump's campaign headquarters show their tattoos with 88 and a Celtic cross on the camera, and the channel did not comment on their significance at all. As you might guess, this was also not an accidental oversight on part of PBS.

"Last night PBS NewsHour ran a report on the Tilly family in Fayetteville, North Carolina. Tillie did not have a history of active participation in politics, but various family members - both old and young - are motivated to vote or start a campaign for the first time for Donald Trump.

If you can throw aside the fact that the Tilly family is campaigning for Trump, this is a small but almost touching story of a family that has decided to take advantage of democracy. Still, if you can throw aside the fact that Grace, one of the main characters of the reportage, wears white supremacist tattoos on both hands.

Above, you see that Grace is agitating on the phone for Donald Trump, with the tattoo of the Celtic cross on her right hand. Despite the fact that the tattoo was clearly visible on the PBS cameras, the report did not say a single word that they are interviewing a walking, racist propaganda bill board. ADL explains that the Celtic cross is one of the most common symbols of white supremacism. Mark Pitcavage, a senior researcher at ADL, tells me:

The Celtic cross is an ancient and revered Christian symbol, usually not associated with extremism. However, one particular version of the Celtic cross - a square cross with a thick circle intersecting with it (also known as "Odin's

Cross") has become one of the most popular symbols of white supremacism. Over the past 20 years, its popularity has not changed, thanks to its use as the logo of Stormfront, the largest website of white racists.

On the other frame, we see Grace's left hand, on which is visible number 88:

On the ADL website, "88 is the secret code for" Heil Hitler ". Finally, a connection was established between Adolf Hitler and Donald Trump.

Pitcavage, who noted that the ADL "does not support or oppose any candidate for an elected office", provided me with examples of the use of these symbols."

Of course, Gawker story is superficial and only hints to supposed relationship od Donald Trump with white extremists without going any deeper.

Grace Tilly with 88 on the left hand

Pete Tilly, Grace's father

Pete Tilly and Donald Trump

On the right of the photograph is the flag with the 1776- the year when secret Society of the Bavarian Illuminati were founded and the year of the Declaration of Independence of the USA. 1776: 2 = 888

"The unmasking book of journalist Michael Wolff about the first year of Donald Trump in the White House" Fire and Fury "was published four days earlier than planned, on January 5, after Trump's lawyers demanded that the publication be canceled and threatened with a law suit after the Guardian newspaper published scandalous excerpts from the book.

"A fire broke out in the Trump Tower in New York, and the video was published by NBC4 New York. The fire occurred on the roof of a skyscraper." According to preliminary information, the reason was a short circuit. "Evacuation was not conducted, no casualties were reported." Reported the same days US news outlets. On the day of the publication of the scandalous book about Trump titled "**Fire** and Fury", of course coincidentally, Trump Tower lights up. A vivid example of media manipulation using numerology and semantics. Date? January 8, 2018. Another coincidence, naturally.

Donald Trump threatens Kim Jong-un with " fire and fury ", of course by chance, on **8.08.17 (888)**

Burning Trump Tower on the day of the release of the book

Behind Clooney's Trump Plaza in "Ocean's '11". Gematria of main villain-Terry Benedict = 888, Donald J. Trump = 888. In the original 1960 film, the character portrayed in the remake by Andy Garcia was called Jack Strager. In the remake his name was changed to Terry Benedict for a numerological match with Donald Trump. All these, of course, accompanied by the code 911, as displayed on safe deposit box. Safe number 2765 =911

Donald J Trump in English Gematria Equals: **888** (d o n a l d _ j _ _ t r u
24 90 84 6 72 24 ^{0} 60 ^{0} ^{0} 120 108 12

Terry Benedict in English Gematria Equals: **888** (t e r r y _ b e n e d i
120 30 108 106 150 ^{0} 12 30 84 30 24 54

Two 8s on van left

2+7=9 6+5=11 911

911 and stylized twin towers on the screen of the computer in casino of Terry Benedict.

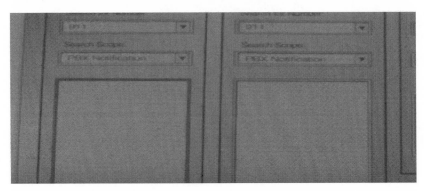

On over 200 pages of this book I only managed to touch superficially on the subject of only 3 codes of 10 known to me to this day. I've attempted to give an explanation of 2 esoteric concepts from several that are currently been identified in my researches. I've had a chance to touch only briefly interesting topic of codes in Shakespeare's works and the cryptographic proofs of their authorship by Sir Francis Bacon. The most convincing explanation of the codes in the films, thousands of high-quality snapshots, graphic materials are required, which greatly complicate and increase the cost of printing any of such publication. For the sake of reducing the coast of printing I had to shorten the presentation to the bare minimum. The author hopes that in subsequent volumes he will be able to deal more closely with those topics that were casually mentioned in this publication or were completely left out of this edition.

Made in the USA
Middletown, DE
26 December 2023

46818741R00149